The Rock from Which You Were Hewn

The Rock from Which You Were Hewn

Created from Dust to Become a Temple of Living Stones

CHRISTINE GRAEF

WIPF & STOCK · Eugene, Oregon

THE ROCK FROM WHICH YOU WERE HEWN
Created from Dust to Become a Temple of Living Stones

Copyright © 2020 Christine Graef. All rights reserved. Except for brief quotations in critical publications or reviews, no part of this book may be reproduced in any manner without prior written permission from the publisher. Write: Permissions, Wipf and Stock Publishers, 199 W. 8th Ave., Suite 3, Eugene, OR 97401.

Wipf & Stock
An Imprint of Wipf and Stock Publishers
199 W. 8th Ave., Suite 3
Eugene, OR 97401

www.wipfandstock.com

PAPERBACK ISBN: 978-1-5326-9051-8
HARDCOVER ISBN: 978-1-5326-9052-5
EBOOK ISBN: 978-1-5326-9053-2

Manufactured in the U.S.A.   March 25, 2020

Scripture quotations taken from the New American Standard Bible®, copyright © 1960, 1962, 1963, 1968, 1971, 1972, 1973, 1975, 1977, 1995 by The Lockman Foundation. Used by permission.

Contents

IGNEOUS
Rock Birthed from Fire and Heat

"Look to the rock from which you were hewn and to the quarry from which you were dug. Look to Abraham your father and to Sarah who gave birth to you in pain." (Isa 51:1–2)

1. Under Earth 3
   "There was a great earthquake." (Rev 6:12)

2. Pressured 12
   "The rock of my strength, my refuge is in God." (Ps 62:7)

3. Weathered 21
   "They were drinking from a spiritual rock which followed them; and the rock was Christ." (1 Cor 10:4)

4. Transported 30
   "There is a time to scatter stones and a time to gather them." (Eccl 3:5)

Contents

SEDIMENTARY
Rock Settles to the Bottom of Water

"You also, as living stones, are being built up as a spiritual house for a holy priesthood, to offer up spiritual sacrifices acceptable to God through Jesus Christ." (1 Pet 2:5)

5. Deposited 41
   "What do these stones mean to you?" (Josh 4:6)

6. Erosion 49
   "Behold, there is a place by Me, and you shall stand there on the rock." (Exod 33:21)

7. Compression 59
   "Then the king commanded, and they quarried great stones, costly stones, to lay the foundation of the house with cut stones." (1 Kgs 5:17)

8. Layered 69
   "There will not be left one stone upon another which will not be torn down." (Luke 21:6)

METAMORPHIC
Morph Means to Change, Transformed

"The earth, from it comes food, and underneath it is turned up as fire." (Job 28:5)

9. Colliding 81
   "Therefore I have set my face like flint." (Isa 50:7)

Contents

10. Transformation 89
    "For no man can lay a foundation other than the one which is laid, which is Jesus Christ." (1 Cor 3: 11)

11. Buried 99
    "So he cut out two stone tablets like the former ones." (Exod 34:4)

12. Emptied 109
    "So with the stones he built an altar in the name of the Lord." (1 Kgs 18:32)

Bibliography 117

IGNEOUS

Rock Birthed from Fire and Heat

Look to the rock from which you were hewn and to the quarry from which you were dug. Look to Abraham your father and to Sarah who gave birth to you in pain. (Isa 51:1–2)

1

Eruption

There was a great earthquake. (Rev 6:12)

DEEP INSIDE EARTH THE rocks spasm and quake the creation. The trembling amplifies as it vibrates through lakes and moves toward the shores, rattling the foundations with a force multiplying as it travels, taking down cities for hundreds of miles around.

Gravity tears at man's structures, turning them to the ground. Every wall collapses. High cliffs crumble into dust. Storms of stars fall through a blackened sky as tens of thousands of people die. Volcanoes erupt shifting Earth's mantle, colliding plates, moving islands out of their places. Tsunamis respond and speed in with great swells of ocean swallowing land.

Cries of devastating terror beg the rocks to "fall on us, hide us!" Filled with the shame of the original fall of mankind in the garden, the recognition of the Lord's voice coming from heaven brings their fear. Iniquity tries to cover itself as people run to hide among the rocks of the mountains, fugitives from their Creator. "Fall on us and hide us from the presence of Him who sits on the throne, and from the wrath of the Lamb" (Rev 6:16). The great day of God's wrath has come. His zeal was declared through visions

of the Lord thundering at the head of his army which is beyond number. The day of the Lord will be dreadful (Joel 2:11).
Who is able to stand? (Rev 6:17).
The radiance of God came to people through Jesus and armed them with the knowledge of his return bringing a time of shaking, a beginning of sorrow as the horror of humankind's immorality culminates in judgment. Nations will rise against each other. Famines will starve the people. Earthquakes will tremble the world (Matt 24:7; Mark 13:8; Luke 21:11).
We will know fully the wrath the Lord has saved us from because of God's mercy.
Heaven stands in awe as an angel at the altar holds a censor in his hand. He takes incense and mingles it with the prayers of those under heaven's altar who have died for the Lord's name. Their prayers are answered as its smoke goes up before God. The angel fills the censor with fire from the altar, and hurls it on the Earth, and there comes peals of thunder, rumblings, flashes of lightning, and an earthquake (Rev 8:3–5).
A third of trees, grasses, and vegetation, the first of God's creations, are destroyed. A mountain of blazing fire is cast into the sea and a third of the sea is destroyed. The Lord's Spirit moved upon the waters to bring about life. It now moves with judgment. A great star burning like a lamp falls into a third part of the fresh water rivers and springs turning them bitter from wormwood. "For My people have committed two evils," the Lord said. "They have forsaken Me, the fountain of living waters, to hew for themselves cisterns, broken cisterns that can hold no water" (Jer 2:13).
A third of the light from the sun, moon and stars is darkened. The harmony of day and night established in Genesis is disrupted. The bottomless pit is opened to unloose imprisoned demons to run chaos and tragedy throughout the Earth. Smoke rises from the pit as if from a furnace. Locusts come out of the smoke prepared for battle. They swarm, bringing the pain of hell for five months. Their stings burn so awfully people try to die but death will not come (Rev 9:1).

Eruption

Angels are sent to release the four angels who are bound in the Euphrates River, the northern boundary of Israel. These have been prepared to slay a third of men (Rev 9:14). The river dries up. Fire, smoke, and sulfur kill a third of the population who are left. The river separated the north from the scene of battle and now an army can march across to assert themselves against God.

Angels are standing attending the throne of heaven with the elders and four living creatures. A great multitude from every nation, tribe, people, and language stand before the throne and the Lamb. Wearing white robes and holding palm branches in their hands, they sing out, "Salvation to our God who sits on the throne, and to the Lamb." They worship before the throne, "Amen, blessing and glory and wisdom and thanksgiving and honor and power and might, be to our God forever and ever. Amen" (Rev 7:9–17).

The ending of the story tells us what our story is about.

It all began in a thunderous creation, under intense pressure, churning up to the surface, breaking pathways across the landscape in a display of meteorites smashing into planets, volcanoes erupting hot molten lava as land appeared. Genesis recounts events of the six days of creation that contain all the mystery of the universe, but does not verify these were twenty-four hour days. The sun does not appear until day four. Passages are measured in the generations of the heavens and the Earth (Gen 2:4; 5:1). The perspective of Genesis looks forward from the Lord laying the foundations when the universe was millions of times smaller, before God expanded its space. Time in the beginning was before the universe stretched.

Then life emerged. In dazzling colors and spectacular shapes, even glowing, rocks beneath our feet tell the story of Earth transforming into riverbeds and diamond rings, giving minerals for technology, sculpting cities and mountains, and layering the epic stories of Earth. Rock would be the element the Lord chose to demonstrate heaven's handiwork. Who is a rock except our God? (Ps 18:31). In the hollow of a rock, rest is found (Gen 49:29). The Lord is my rock, my strength, my deliverer (Ps 18:2). He is a fortress, a force with edges beauty, a space that shelters, a haven of rest, a place to hide. He is the foundation of all things. When judgment was pronounced on a generation that abandoned God, the Lord said, "You neglected the Rock who begot you, and forgot the God who gave you birth" (Deut 32:18). Remember the rock from which you were hewn, the faith of Abraham and Sarah (Isa 51:1-2).

We think of rocks as solid, stopping to pick one up, digging to mine for them, marveling at their uniqueness, round or sharp, composed in all color ranges of pinks and grays, greens and reds. We think of them as unchangeable, hard as a rock. But like Simon, who Jesus called Peter, "Rock" in the masculine, a stone such as is found along a path, believers would go through many changes to be refined out of crystals of different minerals compressed through patterns of light from heights of grace to depths of doubts. When Jesus met the young fisherman, he was saying to Peter, "I know you. I will make you part of the rock of God though you do not yet know it."

"For I am confident of this very thing, that He who began a good work in you will perfect it until the day of Christ Jesus" (Phil 1:6). Jesus sees us as he intends us to be. He sees the work between heaven and Earth transforming our best qualities into faithful stewards. He has prepared a place and is waiting to welcome you and give you some of the hidden manna. Jesus will give you a white stone, and a new name written on the stone that no one knows but he who receives it (Rev 2:17). God implores us to enter his rest: "Give me your heart, my son, and let your eyes delight in my ways" (Prov 23:26). A passionate plea, the Father is concerned for all the prayer rising from this falling world. The psalmist responds, "If Your law had not been my delight, then I would have perished in my affliction" (Ps 119:92). The Lord knows the secrets of the heart (Ps 44:21). He knows that a soul detaching from God is trapped by forces drawing away life.

Recognizing our heart may harden when we don't understand his word, don't believe the people he sends, or how our own ambitions may prevent us from moving into his will, David responded to God with words lifted to heaven asking, "according to your unfailing love, according to your great compassion create in me a new heart, grant me a willing spirit to sustain me" (Ps 51). In heaven when the vials of judgment open and the sound of the trumpet is heard on Earth, men scorched with intense heat curse the God of heaven because of their pain and their sores. They blaspheme as hail of two-foot-wide rocks, weighing a hundred pounds each, fall from the sky (Rev 16:11). They are the unforgiven, counted among those who refuse the only name that can save. They resisted repentance, the step of willingness to be taken through the process of building a rock to stand upon.

When Jesus comes to integrate his people into the expression of God, he is a thunderous wave shaking life into a new creation. In a vision, Isaiah saw the Lord sitting on a throne, exalted, and seraphim standing above him calling to one another, "Holy, Holy, Holy, is the Lord of hosts, the whole earth is full of His glory." The foundations of the thresholds trembled when he called out. The temple filled with smoke (Isa 6:1-4). He thundered on Mount Sinai. Bolts of lightning lit the sky as the holy voice sounded through the galaxies.

The giving of the words of God is compared to teachings dropping like rain, descending like dew, abundant showers on new grass (Deut 32:2). Thunder comes with these rainstorms, awakening us to straighten toward the one who is the giver of life. Rain comes with pleasant fragrance as the ground responds to the nourishment streaming down from above. The wonder of it thundered through the people as the land shook when he came down from far above the stars to give the law in a display of clouds and fire, the sound of a trumpet, and the voice of God. As the trumpet grew louder, Moses spoke and God answered him in thunder (Exod 19:19). The adversaries of the Lord will be broken into pieces; he will thunder in heaven against them (1 Sam 2:10). When he called out, the seven thunders sounded (Rev 10:3-4). When the Son of God died for judgment the Earth quaked and rocks broke apart (Matt 27:51). Again, when he came out of the grave, there was a great quake (Matt 28:2).

Job's heart pounded and leapt when God's voice resounded. "Listen closely to the thunder of His voice . . . God thunders with His voice wondrously, doing great things which we cannot comprehend" (Job 37:2–5). God speaks and with just a word, the mountains fall, Earth is shaken by thunder, volcanoes rumble their fire, and rocks shatter into motion following a cycle like water seeking out the deep places to lift to the sky, carried by the wind to do it again and again. In a great migration continually going into the depths, attaching to other pieces of stone to bring them up to the light, then going back down again, rocks form and reform to compose the land we walk upon.

A planet spinning in space surrounded by the mystery of singing stars reveals a God of communities of renewal. Change can come slowly through hundreds of years or in sudden catastrophes of earthquakes, volcanoes, and manmade explosions. The rock cycle never stops as God orchestrates his oldest element of creation to change each other.[1] A metamorphic rock like gneiss can come from granite, an igneous rock pressured to cause the minerals to line up in distinct bands. Shale, a sedimentary rock, can become slate, a metamorphic rock. If under more pressure, shale turns into a schist that may change into gneiss.

"You send forth Your Spirit, they are created; and You renew the face of the ground" (Ps 104:30).

"[B]e transformed by the renewing of your mind" (Rom 12:2; Eph 4:23).

We feel the rumbling deep within shifting our attention, opening the deep, pushing upward through darkness as the Lord reaches to bring the inner upward into the radiant light, fulfilling its expectant hope and breaking to pieces the surrounding surface that held us captive. We are made from dust. The human body is composed of nature's minerals. Genesis tells us of living beings made of minerals of the clay in the ground, which come from the weathering of rocks. "And the Lord God formed man of the dust of the ground, and breathed into his nostrils the breath of life; and man became a living soul" (Gen 2:7). And out of the ground, God formed every beast of the field and every bird of the sky, and brought them to the man (v. 19). Some days we feel we are nothing

---

1. Villanueva, "How Are Rocks Formed?"

but dust blown by winds. But God's entire intent is to gather dust into stones, beautiful gems formed by weathering and pressures built into an incredible kingdom out of all the tears and unspoken longing.

The mixture of molten rock inside the Earth churns at 2,200 degrees Fahrenheit, crystallizing minerals able to create new horizons. From the realm under the surface magma is pressured until it erupts in fountains of fire moving slow rivers of lava or finds an opening to pour down into Earth's cold crust, melting surrounding rock as it goes. Magma is cooled by air and water to form igneous rock and build a foundation supporting the glorious diversity of plants and animals, sought for building bridges and monuments, floors and colorful countertops. If it cools quickly enough it becomes translucent with shiny glass such as obsidian. Winds come carrying sand and wear particles off the rock. Rushing rivers rub the edges smooth.

Weathering refines the rock, a process our hearts endure as God provides a way for us to transform more deeply. "And let endurance have its perfect result, so that you may be perfect and complete, lacking in nothing" (Jas 1:4). Particles eroding from rocks float around in the water with potential to interact together. Transporting to new places, rivers slow and the rock particles sink to become a new layer of sediment. More sediment builds on top, creating small islands that divert rivers into channels. The weight on the bottom layers cements particles together, creating sedimentary rocks.

"We are afflicted in every way, but not crushed; perplexed, but not despairing; persecuted, but not forsaken; struck down, but not destroyed; always carrying about in the body the dying of Jesus, so that the life of Jesus also may be manifested in our body" (2 Cor 4:8–10).

Over a long time the sedimentary rocks are buried deep under the ground. Again, tectonic plates shift and push them into the fiery heat and pressures change them into metamorphic rock.

"He sends forth His word and melts them; He causes His wind to blow and the waters to flow" (Ps 147:18).

The Rock from Which You Were Hewn

Following him takes us through long experiences to unearth the Lord's buried treasures. Making us from the elements found in Earth, God is completing his workmanship turning us into living stones. Even in the deepest grave, life calls out for meaning that death cannot hold back. He has put eternity in our hearts. There is no plan to save fallen angels who became unpardonable because they had seen the glory of the Lord, knew him and yet chose to walk away. For humanity, emerging into grace where we live and breathe in the presence of the Lord is a series of changes taking us through great darkness, often beneath tremendous pressure into contact with others preparing us as he prepares heaven for us. No matter how deeply we've been pulled into darkness, covered by prevailing sin, his eyes are on the ways of a man, and he sees all his steps (Job 34:21). To the Lord, the night shines like the day (Ps 139:12). He consumes the dark places with the brightness of his being.

"Therefore thus says the Lord God, 'Behold, I am laying in Zion a stone, a tested stone, a costly cornerstone for the foundation, firmly placed'" (Isa 28:16).

Life begins with rock. Science has found the minerals they contain are the spark of all life. In a 2016 interview with mineralogist Robert Hazen,[2] NOVA explained that an experiment mixing and heating basic gases like nitrogen and carbon dioxide did not bring the result that happened when rocks were grinded into the mixture. "The rocks we pick up tell a story: that life couldn't have occurred without rocks," Mr. Hazen said. The atoms reformed into new organic molecules, including amino acids even down on the dark ocean floor, more than a mile below the surface where hot mineral-rich hydrothermal vents support life without sunlight.

The part of the story rocks serve may seem a stretch of barren landscape, yet it is here that gems are created. The tiny grains weathered from ancient rock come to us through time in all shapes and colors organized into a structure, compacting together to make us his living stones. The incredible chemistry of mineral surfaces protect, organize, and template. They take molecules and

---

2. Hazen, "Life's Rocky Start."

concentrate them. The molecules react to form longer and longer structures that supplied both the energy and the mechanism needed in the steps for life's origin.

Construction is a messy process but if everything remains the same in a life, the builder is not present. As Earth attests, continents break apart, oceans form, all from the Lord moving the dust of the ground into rock that shifts the very rationale of our lives. To redeem, the master builder comes in and disrupts all that we find comfortable and familiar. Though we may only want him to fill the empty spaces, our entire reality begins anew through water and wind of the Spirit.

"For thus says the Lord of hosts, 'Once more in a little while, I am going to shake the heavens and the earth, the sea also and the dry land'" (Hag 2:6).

"He who overcomes, I will make him a pillar in the temple of My God, and he will not go out from it anymore; and I will write on him the name of My God, and the name of the city of My God, the new Jerusalem, which comes down out of heaven from My God, and My new name" (Rev 3:12).

"'Yet even now,' declares the Lord, "Return to Me with all your heart, and with fasting, weeping and mourning'" (Joel 2:12).

2

Pressured

The rock of my strength, my refuge is in God. (Ps 62:7)

BELOW THE EARTH WE walk upon, under the soil and stones, far beneath the roots of trees and under the ocean floor, a hard solid compacted layer of granite, limestone, sandstone, and other stone is the bedrock of life on Earth.

Bedrock can extend hundreds of feet deep in the crust or outcrop into mountaintops, rocky coastlines, and quarries. Its rockhead is overlain with weathered stones, soils and sands much younger than the bedrock. Buildings are founded on bedrock, sometimes secured by being drilled to the rockhead. The loose rocks above it cannot support structures that would shift or sink. Engineers trust in bedrock to build secure bridges.

Our lives are rooted in the bedrock. We assume we are deeply anchored but we build on surface concerns, civil rights, personal rights, technology, money investments, education, worldviews of having to gain certain things. Yet still we are left restless, not knowing how to repair our own loneliness. We are Adam and Eve's children seeking our own ways, blaming external forces of society, education, media, even faulting hot summer days. Falling into ineffectual lures telling us that there can be freedom without

PRESSURED

consequence, we only become further enslaved by not believing what God said.

Beneath Earth's bedrock is a thick layer of mantle with chambers of magma, a hot liquid of crystallized minerals and surrounding rocks melting into its heat. When pressure becomes enormous, the magma heaves and seeks release. Pushing upward to find less pressure, magma bursts the confines of the upper mantle, fracturing the rock around it, erupting in fire fountains of liquid rock and molten lava, spewing ash and fumes, changing the entire landscape and air we breathe.

Pressures move through us pushing our anguish up toward heaven and all the hopes breaking in our hearts. Even a faint faith glowing deep within, hoping for God's will to transform a life, "can say to this mountain, 'Move from here to there,' and it will move" (Matt 17:20). It was Isaiah's prayer yearning, "Oh, that You would rend the heavens and come down, that the mountains might quake at Your presence . . . to make your name known" (Isa 64:1–2).

Peals of thunder cracked and rumbled in bolts of lightning as God descended through the heavens, bringing his people up from the depth of their slavery. Deliverance into the kingdom of light came with the thundering at Mount Horeb. Earth trembled. The law was given, the plans for the tabernacle were given, and God inscribed ten commandments on tablets of stone (Exod 19:9–20). Remember that day, Moses said. From the heavens he made you hear his voice (Deut 4:36).

When God moves mountains we hear rocks falling, everything collapsing as he lowers the high places of our own ways and raises the low places that doubted and worried. "'Is not My word like fire?' declares the Lord, 'and like a hammer which shatters a rock?'" (Jer 23:29). The volcanic rush of molten particles become igneous rock, from the Latin word *ignis*, meaning fire. As the burning lava begins to cool it crystallizes, the most important process of mineral formation sustaining life.[1]

We want to move away from the difficult experience, but God's work is to bring a soul to life and bless with a place in his

---

1. "How Did Minerals Form?"

plan. We move into a new struggle needing God to go beyond the nature of earthly impediments, so we must go beyond our own nature.

Four thousand years ago Hagar was taken in as a servant, abandoned without enough money to have a home of her own, the father of her child giving no support. Their lives seemed to move further into darkness as depression, despair, blame, and hopelessness overcame them. Life was not what they had expected as Abraham's wife and firstborn son. Desolate to the unbearable point of accepting death as the only possibility, the anguish of the grave came over them. But the Lord councils us not to lean on our own understanding (Prov 3:5). Wherever we go, he is with us. Even if I make my bed in hell, he is there (Ps 139:8).

Society merges its efforts to address economic hardships and offer support through the struggle, but Hagar's story tells us what God alone can establish. It would be this very anguish that made Hagar a woman privileged to have an angel speak to her twice and bring miracles for her and her child in God's plan to gather the nations in peace.

The Midrash tells of Hagar being a daughter of the pharaoh of Egypt when she saw God perform a miracle to save Sarah from the hands of the Egyptian king during her visit with Abraham. Hagar chose not to stay behind in the idolatry, so she went with Abraham and Sarah as a servant in their household. Sarah was a woman of faith (Heb 11:11), but when she didn't have children she lost trust in God's timing to give her and Abraham descendants. In hopes of creating the blessing, she persuaded Abraham to marry Hagar so they could bring up children.

When Hagar realized she had become pregnant, she acted superior to Sarah, who did not yet have children. Sarah's response was to remind Hagar that she was only a servant by placing harder work onto her. Pregnant and in distress under mistreatment by someone she believed to be God's people, Hagar fled into the wilderness. There was no one to turn to and no one who could change the situation for her. It was the appearance of an angel that calmed her when she was on the way to Shur. He asked her where she was coming from and where she was going.

Hagar explained that she was running away. Heavy with disappointment in life not turning out to be what she planned under the tents where she served, her journey would reveal blessing comes in the Lord's will being done, not her own. As the apostle Paul said, "Shed your old self" (Eph 4:22).

The angel of the Lord told Hagar to return to Sarah and submit to her. Her inner self may have rebelled at such unfair advice, but Hagar was not hardened to the point she could not hear God's voice. She had lived years with the presence of the Lord spoken about in the tents of Abraham and Sarah. The angel soothed her with a promise that she would birth a son whose voice God would hear (*Yishma-El*). He would be a strong man of the wilds and respected among her people. "You shall call his name Ishmael, because the Lord has given heed to your affliction" (Gen 16:11).

Hagar's response was awe. She called God *El Ro'I*, because "I have now seen the One who sees me." In the strength of the angelic message, she went back to Sarah. Hagar gave birth to Ishmael and he lived as Abraham's son for thirteen years before Sarah gave birth to Isaac. Ishmael grew in Abraham's house, where God was revered and angels came and went as guests.

But when Isaac usurped the love of Abraham and Sarah, Ishmael resented him and began to taunt the little boy. Sarah's maternal instinct wanted to be rid of the negative influence that had descended into her home and she insisted that Abraham send them away. Though reluctant, Abraham listened to God, who told him to do as Sarah said. God assured Abraham that Ishmael too would become the father of a great nation.

Abraham had given Hagar and his son only a bottle of water and loaf of bread when they were abandoned to the wilderness. They lost their way near Beer-Sheba. The water had not lasted them long and now they faced a terrible death. Dehydrated and dying, Hagar placed her child in the shade of a bush. She was discarded, unwanted, with no place she belonged. Unable to watch him suffer, she moved away from her child. With no strength left to go another step, Ishmael's name, "God shall hear," was a distant memory.

Everywhere in the Bible tells us that God truly sees each of his people, steps into time and recovers us. He tells the truth of all that has happened to us. Each formed through minerals joining and changing, our new names in white stones hold what only the Lord understands. With the promise never to leave us, he sweeps down from heaven and gives our hardest times a new name. "I'm lost" becomes "I'm found." The faith birthed from the buried turmoils of the innermost heart. We come from churning pressure, in shame not wanting God to look at us. He leads us to look at him and become radiant by gazing upon his beauty. A new vision informs us what we are living for, as it did for John, exiled on the island of Patmos. He sat on the rugged coast with few clothes and little food, downcast and away from his people. Then light thundered into his life, opening a window to the sight of clean white robes where the manna and a new name awaits. It is a spectacular view of the place we are going. Life came to us, imparting a thirst drawn to the beauty of his holiness, waking us to hear his voice speaking endless hope. "I am your healer," he says.

He remembers we are dust (Ps 103:14). The weight of becoming a living stone made from dust presses us into a composite of Abraham's reservoir of faith, Adam and Eve's freedom of choice, Job's misunderstood suffering, and the apostles' brave commitment. It brings us into sight of the two destinations all of humanity will face. "I will destine you for the sword and you will all kneel down to be slaughtered because I called and you did not answer. I spoke and you did not listen." But those who serve the Lord will rejoice and shout for joy with a glad heart (Isa 65:12–14). Jesus confirmed Isaiah's message, saying there are two gates. The wide gate and broad road that many follow leads to destruction. The narrow gate leads to life for the few who find it (Matt 7:13–14).

Again an angel of the Lord is sent to Hagar assuring that God is still listening. Hagar is now seen by a flowing spring of water. She drinks from the well and gives her son water. God tells her that Ishmael has been blessed and that he "will make him fruitful and will multiply him exceedingly. He shall become the father of twelve princes, and I will make him a great nation" (Gen 17:20).

"For You have rescued my soul from death, my eyes from tears, my feet from stumbling. I shall walk before the Lord in the land of the living" (Ps 116:8-9).

Conversation with God begins here, where the innermost recesses of our being look to him to redeem what we cannot fix. The Lord sees that every relationship has a deeper and more complex level than the roles in which a person is cast. Isaiah described his skill not to judge by what he sees with his eyes or decide by what he hears with his ears (Isa 11:3).

The mothers, Sarah and Hagar, both were directed to leave the familiar. They represent a freewoman born through the promise and a bondwoman whose life resulted from decisions of the flesh (Gal 4:24-25). Yet when the soul within is bowed low in defeat, our background does not matter at all. Status and economics are as nothing when angels visit in response to our cry.

In the battle for the inner soul, David turned to the Lord imploring him to "create in me a clean heart" (Ps 51:10). When the Lord sought the king for Israel, he provided the heart in David. It is God who grants repentance (2 Tim 2:25). His touch fortifies with light to give us a heart of flesh (Ezek 36:26). The prodigal returns remembering that he has a father who wants him. David would say it was the spirit of the Lord who delivered him. Paul would say he could do all things in Jesus who strengthened him, praying that we too may be filled to the measure of all the fullness of God (Eph 3:19). Paul, a highly trained scholar of Israel and apostle for Jesus, wrote a testimony of the eternal heart being circumcised, not by human hands but by Jesus in a covenant of blessings through faith working in us (Col 2:11-12).

"In this you greatly rejoice, even though now for a little while, if necessary, you have been distressed by various trials, so that the proof of your faith, being more precious than gold which is perishable, even though tested by fire, may be found to result in praise and glory and honor at the revelation of Jesus Christ" (1 Pet 1:6-7).

The Rock from Which You Were Hewn

The master builder, Jesus, is complimented by his intimate knowledge of each stone and how to work each stone into place. When the Lord directed the temple to be built, it was he who provided the blueprint. The plan is his. The design is his. The gifts he asked to be brought were specific, involving the people's generosity to contribute for God to dwell with them. He drew on the skills of everyone whose heart was willing to fulfill his plan. The craft of stonemasonry built walls to mark durable boundaries so that humanity sees how our Creator places us in the category of holiness.

When we realize God hears us, time begins its passage again. In motion moving rocks out of the way to open tombs, shaking mountains to erupt in desire to be free of human imperfection, cascading rivers to move each particle into place, burying to purify and lift, God speaks again as he did in the beginning. Let there be light and life comes into being. The spiritual soul is drawn upward toward its pure source in the exalted heaven. It is a narrow path, full of valleys and high peaks, through raging storms and calmed seas, entered only in reverencing the Lord (Prov 9:10). Desire for his wisdom brings us through the fire as it did Daniel and his friends. It sustains us through the upheavals as the Lord guards us to refine into spiritual stone, crystallizing cohesive and faithful love for him. Paul's writings to us were empowered from his life absorbing great pressure. So that our own lives are not marred by fear, he asks that we have the full assurance of hope (Heb 6:11). Beyond knowledge of Jesus being a savior to the world, he wants you to have the assurance that he knows you and it is you personally he is saving. In his letter to the Thessalonians Paul is praying in the light of our glorious future in Jesus that every good purpose that is in each of us be fulfilled.

The changes bring a faith that transforms our lives beyond seeing only the surface. When the storm has passed by, the wicked are gone and the righteous stand (Prov 10:25). False thinking is a puff of smoke rising in the collision of storms, but as the soul comes into the benediction of the open air, the colors come back into the world. Countless stars fill the heavens giving testimony to a Creator who cares.

He wants identity to come from the very heart to influence how we perform when the voices come saying we are defeated, we are alone, we should go another way. "The Counselor, the Holy Spirit, whom the Father will send in my name, he will teach you all things, and bring to your remembrance all that I have said to you" (John 14:26). "I have said these things to you, that when their hour comes you may remember that I told you of them" (John 16:4). Remember your identity, or the hardships intended to refine you will confuse you and make you give up. It is here in the hidden inwardness that the Lord brings light to forge decisions of conscience and responsibility that will, collectively, become the standards of community. He is preparing us for the world to come by offering hidden manna that sustains our identity in him.

When Israel saw the manna falling from heaven, they were absolutely certain it was special. But they did not know what this mystery food was so they called it "manna" (Exod 16:15). In Hebrew, the word *mon* means a portion of food. *Mon* is also Egyptian for "what," a word they may have incorporated after centuries living in Egypt.[2] "Manna" means "What is it?" A substance so indescribable and so important it is without definition. Manna brings strength from heaven, beyond our limited abilities.

Breathing, Jesus parts the sea, parts an enemy, clears a holy path by the holy winds of his breath. The splendor of his coming breaks through all the bedrock that was expected to support the plans of life. Jesus says rise, come with him. In the power that can tear down mountains, the tomb opens onto a new path. The rock that prevents us from moving forward is rolled away in lives marked by sacrifice. Lament becomes a soul singing with thankfulness.

The Lord surrounds his living stones with a song liberating them from bondage to take up the narrow path around its turning curves, and down again to the way it leads others upward. The song pulls up waves toward his presence, locks our attention, outdistancing all troubles, always marveling at the Lord as his name is glorified in completing us. The shaken and wordless longings that

2. Posner, "What Does Manna Mean?"

quaked our realities are put to rest as we settle into his presence, in the cleft of the rock where Moses stood watching for him to pass by, the glory shining down, the nearness of the beautiful mystery of him (Exod 33:18).

"He who has an ear, let him hear," Jesus says (Rev 2:17). Hearing is a call to obey. He who obeys is an overcomer, a conqueror, a recipient of the most precious of gifts, the manna and the white stone, a new name that tells the truth about how we have come to be in his kingdom.

"To them I will give in My house and within My walls a memorial, and a name better than that of sons and daughters; I will give them an everlasting name which will not be cut off" (Isa 56:5).

"You have given me the inheritance of those who fear Your name" (Ps 61:5).

3

Weathered

They were drinking from a spiritual rock which followed them;
and the rock was Christ. (1 Cor 10:4)

Rocks pushed to the surface rest on the Earth, but not for long. The winds wear particles off and blow them away. Rushing raindrops rub the rough edges smooth. Water seeps into cracks and freezes. Sun shines on rocks, causing them to expand. Night falls and the rock contracts. Over time this gradually causes pieces of rock to break. Roots of trees spread and pry rocks apart. Ivy grows up around stones, moss surrounds, and rocks are pulled loose. Acid rain dissolves rock and changes compositions.

Stones are ancient, objects at rest requiring a momentum to move them. A planet of abundant water drives the processes of weathering and erosion. Water carries away the minerals, breaking them down into fragments cast into rivers flowing back to the ocean and inland basins. Even beneath the ocean volcanic rocks flow through crevices and break apart.

The result of all this weathering fills valleys and brings mountains and hills low, straightening the crooked, and smoothing the rough roads (Luke 3:5). "I will go before you and make the rough places smooth; I will shatter the doors of bronze and cut through their iron bars" (Isa 45:2). The constant reshaping of even the hardest of rocks displays God's precepts to renew life. "So let us know, let us press on to know the Lord. His going forth is as certain as the dawn; and He will come to us like the rain, like the spring rain watering the earth" (Hos 6:3).

We see him traced in the sky, encountering a beauty so vast, so simple a presence of God that questions are rendered unimportant. Triumph is within sight. Then suddenly the sky fills with clouds and we are lost under a baptism of depression as waters rise over us. Suddenly our lives are being fragmented as the ground shifts and time takes away what we assumed we'd have forever. Yet this is the path into the world to come.

Isaiah described the Lord as having power like a hailstorm and a destructive wind, a driving rain and a flooding downpour. Then hail will sweep away the refuge of lies and the waters will overflow the secret place (Isa 28:2, 17). Job writes: "The falling mountain crumbles away, and the rock moves from its place; water wears away stones, its torrents wash away the dust of the earth; so You destroy man's hope" (Job 14:18–19). The weight of Job's losses was so severe it caused him to want the grave to hide him until the Lord remembered him. "You will long for the work of your hands," he says, confident God's everlasting love would reach for him. "All the days of my struggle I will wait until my change comes. You will call, and I will answer You" (Job 14:13–15).

"I have learned the secret," Paul wrote to believers in his letter to the Philippians (4:12). He did not expect the struggles to be over yet so he reaches forward to what lies ahead (3:13). Through Isaiah, Paul knew the Lord will come to a city lashed by storms, anxious, without comfort. The Lord says he will rebuild it and "set your stones in antimony, and your foundations I will lay in sapphires. Moreover, I will make your battlements of rubies, and your gates of crystal, and your entire wall of precious stones." All the sons will be taught of the Lord and their well-being will be great (Isa 54:11–13). Once tense with betrayals, the citizens will now have trusted friends, tested and tried in the name of the Lord. The Lord speaks to the barren woman, telling her to shout for joy and enlarge her tent because he has family for her as he resettles communities (vv. 1–3). He calls to the sadness of a grieving wife by giving her the greater joy. "For your husband is your Maker, whose name is the Lord of hosts; and your Redeemer is the Holy One of Israel, who is called the God of all the earth" (vv. 5–6).

To forge the path to his rebuilt design, the Lord may change the landscape to become a hedge around us. "I will block her way," he says. Some mountains remain without passage because "She will want to turn back to the life she knew before him, but she will not find what she needs there." This is the affliction that leads his people back onto the narrow pathway. "Therefore I am now going to allure her; I will lead her into the wilderness and speak tenderly to her" (Hos 2:14). "Before I was afflicted I went astray, but now I keep Your word . . . It is good for me that I was afflicted that I may learn Your statutes" (Ps 119:67, 71).

In wrenching aloneness, even an individual grain of sand is still a member of the rock from which it was formed. God can seem beyond reach, far exalted where he dwells in a high and holy place. Yet he is dwelling with the brokenhearted to revive the spirit of the lowly and to revive the heart of the contrite (Isa 57:15). He is found standing steadfast in our sorrows, moving through the pain with us, caring because there is a gain waiting for us. We don't get over loneliness in crowds and groups of people, but by recognizing our connection in the Lord's greater plan. We may reach a time of feeling that no one cares for us or that so much of our world has been lost that we will never recover. He comes to us and delivers from the shallows to recognize that our life is about being an expression of God in this world. Even when no one can possibly understand what we are going through, our lives are not about who is here to understand us. Seeing what it is that God wills for us to be, finding the truth that spans a lifetime reattaches us to God with the comfort of knowing we will eternally have a purpose in God.

Life is lived in both sunlight and in shadows. In each there is a way of prayer. Prayer expresses inspiration, standing tall, full of praise, and ready to meet any challenge when we feel close to God. "The Lord is the stronghold of my life; of whom shall I be afraid?"

(Ps 27:1). And when we feel God is distant, there is prayer that comes from the edge of collapse, weakening as an evening falling at the end of day. "Hear my prayer, Lord; let my cry for help come to you" (Ps 102:1).

Peter, James, and John were brought to the high mountain with Jesus to witness him shining as white as the light as Moses and Elijah appeared and spoke with him (Matt 17:1–3). They filled with the sight of his transcendent beauty. But they did not stay on the mountaintop. After seeing the holy light beneath his cloak of servitude, they were sent into valleys where people were hurting and lost. As we follow further with Jesus, we learn the wonderful feeling of relief as he shows himself faithful in every circumstance. We come to rejoice with him in every circumstance. "O Lord, You have searched me and known me." Even before we speak, he knows our thoughts. Such knowledge is too wonderful, so high we cannot attain to it (Ps 139:1–6). We want to be known. We want to be cherished. God wants us to have that. Follow me, Jesus said to his disciples. I will make you fishers of men. He will make our lives into something meaningful by changing how we view the landscape, able to surpass inhibitions until all our confidence rests in him.

He knows us by a name that no one else perceives. "Come, see a man who told me all the things that I have done," the Samaritan woman drawing water at Jacob's well said to her community. She was not seeking the Lord when Jesus came to her saying, "Everyone who drinks of this water will thirst again; but whoever drinks of the water that I will give him shall never thirst; but the water that I will give him will become in him a well of water springing up to eternal life." Could this be the Messiah? she wondered. Many Samaritans in her town believed in him because of the word of the woman who testified, "He told me all the things that I have done" (John 4:7–39).

He is found by those who do not seek him. He calls many but chooses few. The thief on the cross beside Jesus is in the kingdom simply because Jesus invited him. Condemned in his guilt, he is now called "Forgiven." The separation from heaven is torn by lies set in motion by the fires of hell, a vicious destroyer immediately causing the loneliness of division in family. Corruption settled into incredible darkness, crouching at the gates, crouching within us to destroy the places God desires to dwell among us. We ask that the Lord purify the longings of our heart. It is Hagar's moment of meeting the God who sees her, giving springs of refreshing water, coming to tell her she is still part of his plan.

He is sharing heaven's manna. When Jesus spoke with the Samaritan woman, his disciples were returning from a nearby town with food acceptable for the Judeans. The disciples asked among themselves if perhaps someone already had brought Jesus food. He answered them, "I have food to eat that you do not know about" (John.4:32). Heaven's manna is given to those called to follow the Lord, as the Israelites were called through their wilderness. It looked like a small, round, white seed. Descending before morning light, presented between layers of dew, the bread from heaven encapsulated nutritional needs precisely for the day. It sustained the people of Israel through forty years of wilderness. It is hidden manna, within the hidden life of our heart where only we and the Lord know what is going on, what words have hurt us, the thoughts we have and inner battles that tempt us in deciding to stand in God's will. Manna comes to us when we pray to be certain in each tentative step taken to follow Jesus to his promised world. It comes with tenderness into all the wounded places of our hearts as we become able to allow him close to our hiddenness.

It may seem we're going in circles like the Israelites in the wilderness as Earth keeps spinning us in the atmosphere, but God was preparing a people for a mission. He was teaching them to hear his language when he spoke. He was refining them to shed the old so they would not bring the world's ways into their land. Moses voiced a wish that the Spirit could be on all of them, aligning them each with God's desire. Then the prophet Joel foresaw a time when God would pour out his Spirit on all people. Sons and daughters would prophesy, old men would dream dreams (Joel 2:28).

Thirteen hundred years later the disciples are called to meet the Messiah, who for so long was promised to be full of wisdom, understanding, counsel, might, and knowledge (Isa 11:2). On the day of Pentecost in thanks for the giving of the Torah, the people all praised and lifted up the Lord's name. A rushing wind passed through the room. Jesus breathed the Holy Spirit on his believers and Moses' prayer was answered. The church begins on the brink of something no other people have done. But the future is unknown. The Lord tells us do not be afraid. Perfect love casts out fear. Do not fear, for I have redeemed you; I have called you by name; you are Mine! (Isa 43:1).

The message is that spoken to Israel when the people wanted to return to Egypt, to what they knew. Peter would return to his fishing, afraid and alone after Jesus died. Jesus saw Peter as a rock being gathered with many others to build his church. In his spiritual awakening, Peter would later speak about the cornerstone, Jesus, the church is to be built upon. "Come to him, to that living stone, rejected by men but in God's sight chosen and precious; and like living stones be yourselves built into a spiritual house" (1 Pet 2:4). He quoted the prophet Isaiah, who had told Israel, "Behold, I am laying in Zion a stone, a tested stone, a costly cornerstone for the foundation, firmly placed. He who believes in it will not be disturbed" (Isa 28:16).

Paul spoke of the thirst of his ancestors traveling through wilderness to their homeland. Moses stood by the rock at Horeb and struck the rock. Water flowed from the rock to quench the thirst of all the people (Exod 17:5–6). For they were drinking from a spiritual rock which followed them; and the rock was Christ (1 Cor 10:4). Jesus was struck on the cross for living waters to flow salvation into a thirsting world. He is the foundation stone we are built upon as every testimony is formed from the dust of the ground, sculpted by water and pressure to be placed into his temple, holding up one another, arranged by grace to reflect his image. The Lord's glory dwells here, where we are called to gather. Witnessing the supernatural union of peoples who would otherwise rarely even speak, Paul wrote in Ephesians about his insight into how prayer enables the called to be members of one body. "I kneel before the Father, from whom every family in heaven and on earth derives its name. I pray that out of his glorious riches he may strengthen you with power through his Spirit in your inner being" (Eph 3:14–16). "You who are far away, hear what I have done; and you who are near, acknowledge My might" (Isa 33:13).

The shofar blasts in Israel are a cry to our Father in heaven to help us penetrate his hiddenness. On Rosh Hashanah, the high holy days in early autumn that usher in the ten days of repentance, one hundred blasts of the shofar are based on including the cries of the mother of Sisera, a woman whose name we don't know (Talmud Rosh Hashanah 33b). She waited for her son, a commander in the Canaanite army, to return from battling against Israel. As time passes, she loses hope and begins to weep. Her son was killed (Judg 5:28–30). She was an enemy of the Jewish people, mentioned after Deborah's song of victory. Israel's sages see her as a parent whose grief is so great for the loss of a child that her suffering transcends differences. The shofar cries to the Father on this day with many tears, not only our personal tears, but a summons to hear the sobbing of others. Through the cry of the shofar, quiet desperation is shared and assures that God responds to all our tears. In the shofar blasts we are never alone.

Moses was a lonely man of faith. He died on a mountain alone with God, the way he had begun long years before when he heard God call him from a flaming bush. There are no mourners described to us. No wife or children are at his side. His sister Miriam and brother Aaron have died. Yet his eulogy is unequaled.

> Since then, no prophet has risen in Israel like Moses, whom the Lord knew face to face, who did all those signs and wonders the Lord sent him to do in Egypt—to Pharaoh and to all his officials and to his whole land. For no one has ever shown the mighty power or performed the awesome deeds that Moses did in the sight of all Israel. (Deut 34:10–12)

For each of us there is a river we will not get to cross and a sadness we accept alone. What Moses began, others continued. The heart may long to do a right thing yet never fulfill it. The Lord is so near to our secret thoughts that though the world does not see; he values how we weigh what is good and the inner holy rage at injustices we are helpless to change. David had it in his heart to build the temple, but it would not be for him to do. God said he did well to want that. "But the Lord said to my father David, 'Because it was in your heart to build a house for My name, you did well that it was in your heart'" (1 Kgs 8:18). It was credited to him as righteousness. We may not complete the task God has assigned us to begin, but we are a link in what advances God's will forward. When God first spoke with Abraham, he told him to go, to walk, to pick up his life and turn his footsteps through the dust of other lands. Many footsteps followed his, each taking steps accepting the precepts of God. The steps led into captivity, barefoot walking in Auschwitz, replaced by boot prints of soldiers defending Israel. Dusty shoes, worn shoes, new shoes, walking through the world, standing to defend the knowledge of God's promise, footsteps moving to prevent our steps from going into the lake of fire.

Faith is credited to those who believe his words. "And do not be conformed to this world, but be transformed by the renewing of your mind, so that you may prove what the will of God is, that which is good and acceptable and perfect" (Rom 12:2). Jonah did not feel like going to the Ninevites, a cruel enemy of his people. Yet because of his eventual desire for God's will, an entire community of people turned to God. The mother of Moses had to release her infant by placing him in a basket into the water. Consider Isaiah, who wandered around naked (Isa 20), or Jeremiah, who wore a cattle yoke fastened to his shoulders (Jer 27). Ezekiel ate a scroll that had been given to him then lay down on his side for 390 days (Ezek 1). Believers are chosen to be different as Abraham and Sarah were called into a different life.

The decision is to care more about what God thinks than what others think. We are warned, "How can you believe, when you receive glory from one another and you do not seek the glory that is from the one and only God?" (John 5:44). It is to "he who has an ear, let him hear what the Spirit says to the churches" that gains the white stone with a new name (Rev 2:17). The greatness of Moses was in how his life demonstrated care for his people coming out of his relationship with God. We are as great as the purpose we serve and we all can serve because the same divine presence that sustained Moses calls to us with a plan.

This is deliverance. God has prepared us for this, even as the elements of our lives in the world weather and fade. As a particle of the infinite, human life is as valued as the infinite. The pathway to the kingdom is God's hand crafting vessels able to hold light so we can claim a sanctity that is ours forever. Even when we may not feel near to the Lord, when prayer won't come and kindness is far from thought, there is the gift of his words to keep us in his framework. The deeds the Lord instructs us to keep enjoin our heart if we wait for overwhelming emotions to settle as we keep within his instructions.

The wisdom of Solomon included even death in the seasons apportioned to us to experience. There is a time to give birth and a time to die (Eccl 3:2). As we let go of the hand of loved ones, surrendering them to angels to carry back to God, death to a believer is a narrow path into a sunlit world because the Lord's rage against this theft of life caused him to defeat it in songs of victory. We will all lose our strength. Eyesight will dim. Beauty will fade. All will lie in a grave because of the many things that cause a heart to stop beating. The example of Abraham, Moses, prophets, and apostles communicates to us the priority of God. Pursue life. The only factor that matters is that we end still free in the Lord's perfect will, proclaiming the invitation of God's mercy. Even at the end of his journey, ready to die, Moses directed the people to be courageous.

"The Lord your God is the one who goes with you. He will not fail you or forsake you" (Deut 31:6).

4

Transported

There is a time to scatter stones and a time to gather them. (Eccl 3:5)

WATER AND WIND CARRY off fragments of igneous rocks, rolling tiny particles in streams and large boulders in fast-moving rivers, dissolving minerals, bumping stones against each other to break off pebbles, or blowing gravels and dust off hilltops, sorting into particles that will combine into sedimentary rocks such as shale, mudstone, and siltstone.

Set in motion when God first spoke into the elements, igneous rocks cover the Earth with topography, inviting the life of plants and trees and sweeping entire lives away from the familiar into the new by his Spirit. Sedimentary rocks form from these fragments of old rocks. Touched by the atmosphere and dissolved salts in the ocean and rivers, new minerals are formed, new passageways opened to extract and combine the particles.

Constantly shaping and unshaping each introspection, the foundation a life is built on must be broken down to expose falseness and be rebuilt on the cornerstone of Jesus, heir to all things. Tumbled through right and wrong perspectives until we inwardly understand the path we are to choose, for a time we are content, then tumbled again as life is shaken and we fall from high cliffs into despair. Political correctness, doing good deeds, being a nice person busy with activities, conformed through peer contagion—all are social norms built on sand. The cornerstone of Jesus is repentance and all that God says is truth. In the downpour, in the rushing currents that reshape lives comes healing rains intent to transform by carrying away what prevents us from becoming one with his chosen.

The waters rise over us as they did Jonah. Jonah realized the fish that swallowed him was his deliverance and he prayed. There in the deep, out of sight of the others in the boat, he turned toward the Lord and the Lord brought him to fulfill his calling. The Lord is directing lives to come together forming his body, propelling us through floods to be brought to an appointed place with others. In his name he sent them out by twos to permeate the world with light. If one falls down, the other can help him up (Eccl 4:10). Also in his culture a word was established by more than one witness. He gave them authority and he gave them each other. Equipped with the armor of his words, the simplicity of being unencumbered by material clutter, and his anointing from heaven that no man's institution can endow, they did what Jesus did and proclaimed what he proclaimed.

They anticipated hostility along the way. Jesus had told them there will be places that do not want to hear, places Jesus himself is rejected. He says to move on and shake the dust off their feet (Mark 6:11). Reverent Jews would shake the dust from their feet when leaving Gentile territories to show their separation from heathen practices. Disciples shaking off the dust of a town showed their separation from those who rejected the Messiah. Wherever the disciples offered salvation and it was accepted, believers were sealed in heaven. Wherever the message was rejected, unbelievers had no standing in heaven. "Whatever you bind on earth shall have been bound in heaven; and whatever you loose on earth shall have been loosed in heaven" (Matt 18:18). Weary, frightened, laden with worries, the early band of believers remembered his divine power, knowing that he will fulfill every vision spoken of him. "For You have been a defense for the helpless, a defense for the needy in his distress, a refuge from the storm, a shade from the heat; for the breath of the ruthless is like a rain storm against a wall" (Isa 25:4).

Each step overwhelmed in wind storming against a wall presses us on a narrow path. The narrowness constricts, almost choking in the thick oppression that comes when we won't bow to the powers ruling the world. Afflicted, mistreated, confused by what was once considered dependable suddenly shifting, and we are sent reeling away from all that was familiar. Shattered dreams leave us hollow; a career we thought we'd have is not possible and we have to accept it is never going to happen; the one we love the most walks out on us; a health problem limits our achievements; peers reject us for choosing to follow God's way—all can result in being pressed into uneasy pathways. The world spins into pieces but God does not move. He has told us his name. He was and is and always will be. He is the source of all being. He is listening for us to come to him and say, "This is painful; this was important to me; I am feeling like who I am and the gifts I think I offer do not matter at all in this world."

Each time we see Jesus he is responding to those in the constricted places, those whose world has narrowed in on them. Though it seemed to Paul that he and his companions had been displayed as a spectacle, the Lord's compassion is all through Scripture, telling us he is for us, wanting us to triumph.

Heaven witnesses the magnificent process and records the transformations happening in the world. The angels were looking upon them (1 Cor 4:9).

When we expect certain things, such as someone I marry will make me happy, if I make more money I'll be happy, or if I follow Jesus nothing bad will happen to me, we will pivot into a confused direction because what Jesus said is that in the world we will have trouble. He sends the Comforter to us but our tears will not be completely redeemed until he returns to reign (Rev 21:4). When we are heavily discouraged we think failure is all we have, but it is not all. We have his understanding. We have his plan. We have him. If we expect what Jesus has told us, we won't be shattered when the erosions of a life leave us with nowhere to turn. It is a narrow path framed by God's instructions and laid with memorials of the voices of those who went before us.

Days before the Israelites are released from enduring centuries of exile in Egypt, Moses speaks to them. There had been wondrous signs and devastating plagues and they are ready to leave. Moses does not talk to them about the land God has given them. He does not speak about the journey they face going through a desert. He addresses the people about teaching children the story of what God has done when the events become a distant memory. He emphasizes the importance, repeating it three times (Exod 12:25–27; 13:8, 14).

He speaks to a people with children and grandchildren who will be exposed to a world of pagan practices when they enter a new region. He wants them to preserve identity embedded in conversations of the powerful hand of God constant and immutable interceding for us. It is this link between generations that preserves the identity of an entire nation. The youth coming up behind them will know they are members of a people whom God rescued. They will know they have a purpose in this world to honor the freedom and knowledge that God gifted them.

If we lose the story, the youth lose a sense of family and collective heritage that connects them to the past and to a future shared with others. In the Middle Ages identity was based on religion, but religion led to war between Christians and Muslims, Protestants and Catholics. Then attempts were made to focus on observations of philosophy and science, teaching that all men are to be brothers. Identity pushed itself forward in the Aryan race and class struggles under Stalin. The result was the killing of a hundred million people.

The modern world then emphasized the individual identity, dissolving shared values for the right of individuals to do or be anything they choose. At intersections where God's story may be carried forward, contemporary thinking detaches from encounters with God's wondrous deeds. The result is people becoming particles of dust blowing in every wind, unattached from transforming into a rock the Lord can use. When you know who you are and why you are here, the journey through God's wilderness is taken with confidence. Children who are heirs to the story are connected to the people who made it possible for them to be here because of what God meant to them. Moses was speaking of the important gift that would transform the world.

We pick up the stones along the way, holding them, studying them, searching for a way through the narrow gate. The weeks that preceded the destruction of Jerusalem and the temple are called *Bein HaMitzarim*, the narrow place or between the narrow straits after the verses of Jeremiah. When Judah went into exile under affliction and harsh servitude, having to dwell among other nations, she found no rest. Pursuers overtake her in the midst of her distress (Lam 1:3). Our efforts become insignificant. Our fight to do things in our own way is over.

It is a vulnerable time exposed to enemies while crossing to reach another place. It is a time of displacement and loneliness. The fast of this mourning is first mentioned in Zechariah 8:19 as a day marking tragedy that only Jesus will transform into joy. It is a somber interval, as in grieving a death, because Jerusalem's walls were under siege and prayer in the temple could no longer continue. Such somberness is only a pause in the rhythm of the Lord's leading to remind us to minimize self and recognize the mosaic of day-to-day blessings with appreciation of the wonder of God's promise. Because the Lord will redeem our joy, Zechariah said to love truth and peace. We have unending sacraments of joy with God's Son. Even when our path is constricted, we remain inside the Lord's plan. The first great song of Scripture comes out of a narrow pathway to fill the sky with song lifted from thanking the Lord for his legacy of triumph (Exod 15:1–21). Melodies of praise are markers along well-worn paths of tears because God never abandons us. "Do this in remembrance of me," Jesus said as he broke bread with his disciples during Passover. "Remember you were slaves," Moses said to his people (Deut 15:15).

For the soul to lift us in inspiration, we want happiness both in the present moment and the future. The Lord has given us both. List blessings we do have—legs to walk with, artistic or musical talent, family, parents, a friend, a home, hands to work with—and compare it with a wish list of cars, boats, more clothes and money. It becomes apparent the blessings we have already been given are most important and it is these we most want carried into the future. He's given us optimism for the future, a steady flow of gladness that empowers energy from knowing we will accomplish what the Lord has set before us. He's given us the sense of permanence we are looking for and the knowing that our growth in his wisdom makes a difference in the lives of others. The manna he gifts us is complete.

When there is no more strength and life is taking us where we'd never choose to go, it would be easy to give up and let go. Survivors carry so much pain. When God is silent prayer won't come easily. But the invitation from heaven is to follow him through times of dancing and times of clarity into times of solitude so gripping that we hear nothing anymore. God's silence tells us to wait. Draw nearer, seek him. Open the Scriptures to know what he says. "And I will be a father to you, and you shall be sons and daughters to Me" (2 Cor 6:18). His Scripture brings us to recognize him when he is speaking and know where we fit into the bigger picture he is piecing together. You will lose the battle if you get impatient and look to other sources. Ecclesiastes 1:14 says, "I have seen all the works which have been done under the sun, and behold, all is vanity and striving after wind." The power to save comes from above the sun, in the highest heaven, where God dwells in holy light. He may be quiet at times, but his light is eternally sovereign.

No one can untangle the microscopic changes that create entirely new stones except God. But we can approach God's throne to receive grace to endure the transitions into becoming living stones (Heb 4:16). The mysterious way the Lord brings good outcomes from a world filled with evil when all the elements are mixed, the weeds and wheat tangled together, brings all through time to preserve what is his own and fulfill his glory. How he does this is beyond our comprehension. We cannot fathom the reasons someone suffers, the hardships in the lives of the prophets and apostles, even God's own Son. God has mercy on whom he wants to have mercy, and he hardens whom he wants to harden. Someone will ask, then who is able to resist his will? But who are you, being human, being the clay in God's hands, to talk back to him and question his will? (Rom 9:17–18). "'For my thoughts are not your thoughts, neither are your ways my ways,' declares the Lord. 'For as the heavens are higher than the earth, so are my ways higher than your ways and my thoughts than your thoughts'" (Isa 55:8–9).

The Lord distinguishes the innermost identity of each person, telling Abraham to go from his country, his national identity, and from his birthplace that ingrains with identity (Gen 12:1). He was told to go in pursuit of God and in that journey he found himself. Abraham discovered his soul's transcendent light sparked with the inspiration of God's holiness coming into his life with a force that would later lift an entire people out of Egypt's house of bondage (Exod 20:2). We cannot try to explain why certain things happen and others do not. The world rejected its Creator and became a place where the saddest of things happen. The question to ask is, "Lord, what do you want me to learn?" Even fully knowing the glory of the destiny of his believers, Jesus still wept at the death of Lazarus. He cried because it is grievous to lose a loved one. It hurts. He understood our mourning. What we learn is that he set us free to cry when our heart breaks and know that the tears will dry. "I will see you again, and your heart shall rejoice, and no one will take your joy away from you" (John 16:22).

The prophets struggled with depression, unfaithful spouses, and broken communities. To God, it was not about the issues they struggled with but their response to turn their hearts to follow God when they heard his voice. God has tied his name to them, to Abraham, Isaac, and Jacob, to the Gentile prostitute who saved Israel, the widow who opened her door to Elijah, and the many whose allegiance to the Lord is shown in willingness to let their lives be carried by the Holy Spirit, trusting as God led to live in a tent, build an ark, cross a deep river. It required the Lord to transport minerals to create the highly valued marble beneath the white, coarsely crystalline limestone that God instructed be used to build the temple. Though the world may not discern it, the Lord has handpicked each stone for a unique purpose, fit together into his design to display his presence among us. To be children of Abraham and Sarah is to hear the call of God taking us through narrow passages. When Moses and his people sang after the splitting of the sea, the children of Israel were born into a nation. It is the place where the singers are made into one new body with song carrying through Earth's highest atmosphere and its lowest defeats.

Our own stories are still being written. Whatever setbacks we have encountered or missteps we have taken, faith is alive, living and growing, sometimes slowly, always a part of him. Stones may change purpose with changing circumstance. Found buried for preservation and safekeeping or unintentionally discarded by time, stone carvings from Viking days, Crusader castles, and Anglo Saxon cultures found in piles of rubble are repurposed into horse troughs, blocks in church walls, and monuments in garden parks. The skills of stonemasonry design beautiful shapes, leaves and flowers, words, and symbols. Granite is a hard stone solidified far underground, requiring great persistence in its common use in many Cornish churches and its durability as curbstones. The strong thick walls of castles such as the White Tower of the Tower of London began being built in 1070 from sedimentary stone like limestone and sandstone. Metamorphic marble is carved into statues and for the facing on many Byzantine and Italian Renaissance buildings. The Greeks used it to mold images of Socrates and Plato.

During its life a piece of stone has served many people in many ways. Removed from its contextual use, a carved stone, even a coin, is just a stone. Its significance in one community is lost to the meaning of the next. No longer altarpieces or signage for an entrance, they are repurposed into a new relevance. A molded block from an old building becomes important for its sentiment in its reuse as a grave marker, more emotionally valued than the knowledge of it being carved a thousand years ago by an unknown craftsman. It may become a museum piece, detached from any of its uses.

Every stone becomes changed as the handiwork of God advances his kingdom. The marks each stone carries remind us of all it comes through, events along the way that formed and unformed its uses. Stones in Israel bring remembrance of the priests and prophets and God's everlasting presence. When the second temple in Jerusalem was destroyed by the Romans, they threw down many of the big stones from on top of the plaza to the street below. The supporting walls have remained standing for more than two thousand years, radiating the promise that the people will return to their land. Families who survived fled to other places. Twenty-four families of *kohanim* (priests) settled around Galilee. Three families of priests came to live in the village of Peki'in high on a mountaintop in Galilee. A synagogue was built to serve as a house of study, displaying two stones that the priests are said to have brought from the destroyed second temple.

Even the stones witness to the expression of God's work to be done in all the Earth; everywhere hearts are beating. With the skills of a master, he refines us and molds every experience into a song of his glory.

SEDIMENTARY

Rock Settles to the Bottom of Water

You also, as living stones, are being built up as a spiritual house for a holy priesthood, to offer up spiritual sacrifices acceptable to God through Jesus Christ. (1 Pet 2:5)

5

Deposited

What do these stones mean to you? (Josh 4:6)

AT THE BEGINNING OF creation tiny creatures with hard shells crawled along the bottom of the ocean, taking in huge amounts of calcium that washed down from stones. When they died their hard shells sank and settled on the ocean floor. Sand in the water washed over, scraping the shells into white dust, mixing with the remains of countless other creatures and the calcium dissolving into water. Over geological time the shells piled into thick layers rich in calcium from the igneous rocks. Pressed together under many layers, igneous particles assemble to become sedimentary rocks.

When God separated the water and dry land and rock was exposed, he planted a garden in Eden. Then the year-long global flood of Genesis 6–9 divided the Earth's geology into pre-flood, flood, and post-flood rocks. The pre-flood rocks of Israel are found in the Elat area in the far south of the country. The rising waters transporting sediments to deposit over the continents left layers in Israel, testifying in the sandstone and pebbles at the base of the flood and the massive fine-grained chalk from the shells of such minute marine organisms as foraminifera, coccoliths, and rhabdoliths in beds at the top.

Waters receded, exposing stone made from the decomposed shells of ancient life mixed with minerals. The plates of Earth's crust collided in powerful tectonic upheaval, pushing the bottom of the sea up, thrusting sediments to build higher hills and uplift the Judean Mountains standing north to south. Jerusalem sits on top of this ridge. Earth's plates pulled apart, splitting mountains and carving deep rifts to open the Red Sea and the quiet valley of the Dead Sea and Jordan River. Noah began to newly establish mankind. After many lives, God told Abraham to leave his homeland and follow a path to a place God would show him. Abraham with his flocks and his nephew Lot walked down into the valley created by the flood that made a great rift in the mountains extending to Africa. He walked down to where the River Jordan flows and walked up into the hills of Samaria, walking along the limestone crust of the mountains made by the shells of the tiny sea creatures.

The command from God would move another life, a woman named Hagar, from her home into the unknown. She was a stone slipping silently through the water in a despair so deep she waited for death. And a young man named Joseph was sent from his family and sold into slavery. A prophet named Jeremiah found himself sinking in mud at the bottom of a cistern.

"Deliver me from the mire and do not let me sink; may I be delivered from my foes and from the deep waters" (Ps 69:14).

Stones are stationary, sinking into Earth until a force moves, such as the flow of a mountain stream during a spring flood. As rivers deepen, their current slows and the rock fragments mixed with soil and dust dropping from the wind sink to settle in layers. Sediments accumulate. Rocks get buried. We may feel pressed to the outer edge of all suffering, so far from light that we wonder, how can we get back to God? There is no getting out of the powers of hell by man fighting against his own nature. But it is only the shadow of death we pass through. A message of liberation came to Hagar when the Lord told her she would have a son who would be as wild and free as the donkeys roaming the desert hills. The Lord sought out Joseph before he was taken into captivity and gave him a dream that meant he would be a leader of the family. All through his prison term and famine he held the divine knowledge that he was to unite his brothers.

When he became viceroy of Egypt, Joseph could have sent messengers to his father to tell him he was still alive. But he had the deeper concern that the Lord had shown him. When his brothers came to him, he orchestrated a challenge to see if his brothers had learned to stand together. Judah passed this challenge by offering himself as a slave in place of his brother Benjamin. Only then did Joseph reveal himself and told them to rush and tell his father he was alive (Gen 45:9, 13). In the first recorded moment in which one human being forgives another, the nation of brothers was reunited.

Jeremiah was the prophet born in Anathoth, about three miles north of Jerusalem, whose ministry extended for more than forty years. Full of warnings, grieving, imprisoned, captive, and laughed at, Jeremiah was given assurance of the future. "O Jacob My servant, do not fear, Nor be dismayed, O Israel! . . . Jacob will return and be undisturbed and secure, with no one making him tremble" (46:27). When he had been imprisoned because of foretelling that the city would fall, Jeremiah 32 tells how he redeemed a piece of land to keep in his family, an act of conviction placed in the days to come God promised his people.

"He sent from on high; He took me; He drew me out of many waters" (Ps 18:16). The journey out of the desert can weary us. At times we see little progress. It helps to revisit the beginning where we felt we were sinking beyond reach and recognize all that the Lord has walked with us through to deliver and change us. After twenty years, Jacob returned home to Canaan. He had left fleeing in fear from his brother Esau. During his flight he stopped to spend the night at Bethel in the Judean Hills. It was here that Abraham had built an altar to God and called on his name (Gen 12:6–8), and here the place his father Isaac was bound for sacrifice.

Jacob dreamt he saw a ladder reaching to heaven with angels of God ascending and descending on it. A voice spoke to him, assuring him of God's protection and affirming the promise that the land he was resting on would be given to him and his descendants. When he woke in the morning, Jacob took the stone that he had rested on, made it a sacred pillar, and poured oil on it as a thanksgiving. He called the place Bethel, home of God.

Years later when he returns to Canaan he is no longer alone. He comes with wives, children, and a wealth of goods. God had told him to return to Bethel, where he had erected the single stone altar to God acknowledging their communion. Jacob had vowed, saying, "If God will be with me and will keep me on this journey that I take, and will give me food to eat and garments to wear, and I return to my father's house in safety, then the Lord will be my God. This stone, which I have set up as a pillar, will be God's house, and of all that You give me I will surely give a tenth to You" (Gen 28:20–22).

The Lord sends him back to where he began, giving him the opportunity to realize all that has happened to change his life during the past two decades. God reminds him that Bethel is the place he "appeared to you when you fled from your brother Esau" (Gen 35:1). Knowing this as a holy place, Jacob anticipates a meeting with God and he builds an altar this time with many stones. The single stone was a creation of God symbolizing his kindness in coming to Jacob. The altar of many stones was assembled by Jacob, involving his own hands in an act to fulfill God's will and bring himself closer to God.

Jacob is still in fear of Esau and prays to the God of his fathers, Abraham and Isaac. Jacob says, "I am unworthy of all the loving kindness and of all the faithfulness which You have shown to Your servant; for with my staff only I crossed this Jordan, and now I have become two companies" (Gen 32:10). He reminds God of his promise to prosper him and make descendants to number like the sand of the sea. Thinking to pacify Esau, he sends his servants with hundreds of animals—goats, lambs, cows, bulls, and donkeys—to meet his brother. Jacob remained alone in the camp. A stranger appeared and wrestled with Jacob into the deep blue night. Hosea 12:4 describes Jacob's opponent as an angel: "Yes, he wrestled with the angel and prevailed; he wept and sought His favor. He found Him at Bethel and there He spoke with us."

In a tense conflict, Jacob entwined with the angel, arms wrapped, gripping each other, and the angel lifted a hand to reach to strike the upper joint of Jacob's thigh. Seeing that he could not defeat Jacob, he says, "Let me go, for dawn is breaking." As morning light rises on Jacob, Jacob said, "I will not let you go unless you bless me." Then the angel said, "Your name shall no longer be Jacob, but Israel; for you have striven with God and with men and have prevailed" (Gen 32:21–28). All of Israel emerged victorious as Jacob came through the struggle glowing in the sun's light, leaving his old self behind and becoming anchored to heaven when God gave him part of his name, Elohim.

"I love the Lord, because He hears my voice and my supplications" (Ps 116:1). "Therefore we have confidence to enter the sanctuary" (Heb 10:19).

When God laid the Jordan he piled rocks from beneath the ocean to rise high above the valley, sloping to spread into the arid eastern desert sands. After a long time under the pressure of layers, the particles and fragments cemented together into sedimentary rocks, preserving stratified stories of continental plates shifting. Pushing up magma that pushed up sediments and stones marked by oscillating ripples of water gave minerals to make the land bloom.

The Jordan flows through the history of the Bible, carrying minerals and sands southward into the Sea of Galilee and meandering to empty into the stillness of the Dead Sea. Jordan lies at a tectonic crossroads. The heat in the Earth slides the Arabian Plate north and east, one of three continental plates—the African, Arabian, and Indian Plates—that have been moving northward and colliding with the Eurasian Plate to push up the Zagros Mountains of Iran, drawing rocks down into the Earth and setting the scene for plates to collide in potentially dangerous earthquakes, tsunamis, and volcanoes. A fault wends its way from the Dead Sea along the Jordan River.

The Israelites crossed here from slavery in Egypt into freedom when they made the journey across the Jordan on dry ground. After the nation had crossed, God instructed Joshua to have twelve men from every tribe get twelve rocks out of the river from where the priests' feet had stood and carry them over to lay on the riverbank where they would camp (Josh 4:2). Twelve stones were piled high on the west bank of the river at Gilgal as a remembrance for all generations to look upon and recall the Lord's faithfulness. When Israel's children ask in times to come what the stones mean, tell them that "the waters of the Jordan were cut off before the ark of the covenant of the Lord" (Josh 4:6–7).

Then Joshua set twelve stones in the middle of the river in the place where the feet of the priests bearing the ark of the covenant had stood until everything was finished that the Lord commanded Joshua, according to all that Moses had commanded Joshua. Scripture says the stones are there beneath the water to this day (Josh 4:9–10). When the priests with the ark came up from the river and stepped onto dry ground, the waters of the Jordan returned to flowing as they had before (v. 18).

The rocks beneath the river's water give an account in an eternal perspective of salvation. Joshua's given name at birth was Oshea, which means salvation. Moses added an abbreviation of the covenant name, Yahweh, to Oshea, expanding it into Yehoshua, Joshua in English, which means "God is salvation" (Num 13:16). The twelve stones are a memorial and a promise of being saved and lifted from the waters of judgment. Moses represented the law that could not cross into the promise of the world to come. Jesus, born under the law (Gal 4:4), was empowered to complete the task. The ark typologically points to Jesus standing in the midst of judgment to hold back the waters, where twelve stones were placed, and allowing stones to be brought up and delivered to the shore as a sign (Josh 4:6). When those in times to come look upon the name of Jesus and ask what he means to us, we are to tell them how he called us out of enslavements, held back judgment, and made a path to bring us into new life so that "we all with unveiled face, beholding as in a mirror the glory of the Lord, are being transformed into the same image from glory to glory, just as from the Lord, the Spirit" (2 Cor 3:18).

Each time the life of one of the Lord's people was dislodged and sent to follow a new path, the power in heaven became more than a Creator. God became our Father. Remembering the place we are from, where we crossed over and the shackles fell to the ground, we come to see ourselves as God sees us, dearly loved, a needed part of his body, grieved over when walking wrong ways, specifically created for a good work assigned to us since the foundation of Earth.

Like stones deposited in water, we sink and, like minerals composing a new stone, grace meshes our qualities with others, anointing each with a gift that sends us forward. "So we, who are many, are one body in Christ, and individually members one of another" (Rom 12:5). Each stone is a living testament withstanding the onslaught of false messages. What we have been given is a jewel much more precious than the world we devote so much attention trying to put a boundary around. If we don't erect boundaries around spiritual gifts, commitment to the Lord's values will erode. The pressures from daily assaults are too strong. Spiritual knowledge brings great walls with ability to keep shared words growing in stories that tell of humility, gratitude, charity too precious to leave unprotected. True faith lives in relation to God's interests on Earth, taken to his mountaintop to see his far-reaching plan and told to abide in his word even when our lives seem to be sinking. Gifts can soon become meaningless without the knowledge that is connected to God's higher purpose.

The voices of history echo through us to help our own voice. We're shown Moses approaching God asking to be shown his ways, adoring God, in the strength of their friendship. As he got closer and stood before God, his own limitations became more evident to him. He was made more humble than anyone on Earth (Num 12:3). David wrote that the sacrifice the Lord wants is a humble spirit. The battle is in the struggle to come nearer to God and accept the power is in his hands. In his conversation with the Lord in Exodus 33, Moses sets the example of how to speak with God. "Let me know Your ways that I may know You, so that I may find favor in Your sight. Consider too, that this nation is Your people" (v. 13). His heart seeks God's will above his own, for himself and on behalf of his people, because his life is irrevocably connected with theirs through God's love for them. His prayer seeks knowledge—that he may know God.

More immediate than any other need, he asks for God's presence as the remedy. "If Your presence does not go with us, do not lead us up from here. For how then can it be known that I have found favor in Your sight, I and Your people? Is it not by Your going with us, so that we, I and Your people, may be distinguished from all the other people who are upon the face of the earth?" (vv. 15–16). The only hope to escape tyranny and be washed clean is to enter a new kingdom and gather under the king who will shepherd us. God responds by blessing Moses. And the Lord said to Moses, "I will also do this thing of which you have spoken; for you have found favor in My sight and I have known you by name" (v. 17). Moses' response is to want more of God's presence. Moses said, "I pray you, show me your glory" (v. 18).

We are so close to the unapproachable light blazing from heaven, we are standing with angels praising him. The writer of Hebrews reminds that worship on Earth is at one with worship in heaven, where angels sing, "The whole earth is full of his glory" (Isa 6:3). "You have come to Mount Zion, to the city of the living God, the heavenly Jerusalem. You have come to thousands upon thousands of angels in joyful assembly" (Heb 12:22).

Our entire lives are full of his glorious presence in the many ways he has guided, bestowed understanding, provided, and given an anticipation of heaven. Therefore encourage one another with these words, Paul, said to set our minds on things above because our lives are hidden with Jesus in God. We will appear with him in glory when he appears (Col 3:2–4).

6

Erosion

Behold, there is a place by Me, and you shall stand there on the rock.
(Exod 33:21)

SPRINGS OF WATER SEEK the cracks between rocks and begin to hollow out more rock to let in air. Sea caves form by water coming in powerful waves, breaking off slabs of rocks, smoothing walls as they wash in and out, grinding sand against the rock to produce strange and beautiful offerings. Flowstones develop translucent curtains from a steady flow of water down sloping walls. Stalactites drip limestone from their roofs into chandeliered deposits hardening and extending over years. From the floor stalagmites rise up as mineral-bearing water drops from the roof of the cave. Pillars of hard rock form when stalactites and stalagmites meet. Or, defying laws of gravity, helictites grow in twisted curling helixes.

There are many kinds of caves, each telling the story of how geology is shaped by nature's interactions over countless centuries. They present the paintings our ancestors left in lines of soot burned into walls. They have been a cradle to humanity, shelter, storage rooms, museums to house the testaments of lives, and places of sanctuary to gather and pray. The abundance of caves around the globe is provided by rocks and the elements to shape them found nearly everywhere. Most of the world's caves form in limestone. Limestone, made from generations of coral, shells, and zooplankton fused into solid rock, is susceptible to acids, which break up the calcium carbonate into calcium compounds. A bedrock of limestone is an ideal place for nature to carve out a cave.

Trickling water through the cracks, drop by drop God forms channels, dissolving stone to release elements needed to make more carbonic acid to expand the cavern. The flow creates caves at various depths and may carve an underground river through a mountainside, creating entrances to the outside. Within many of Israel's mountain ranges God has hollowed incredible secret caves, linking some by tunnels and hidden springs. He has put cover in place by stretching out rocks that would be sought for a hiding place. "For in the day of trouble He will conceal me in His tabernacle; in the secret place of His tent He will hide me; He will lift me up on a rock" (Ps 27:5). The attribute most identified with Jesus is the inward quiet he brings us into, the Rock of Ages.

When Moses asked the Lord to "teach me your ways, show me your glory" in Exodus 33, he was asking God to make sense out of his situation. "You say to me, 'Bring up this people!' But You Yourself have not let me know whom You will send with me," he says (v. 12). The Lord said to come, "There is a place near me where you may stand on a rock" (v. 21). The encounter in the cleft of the rock restored Moses with renewed purpose. Elijah later comes to the mountain and seeks shelter in the rock of a cave. He was weary, emptied, and needed time apart to replenish physically, emotionally, and spiritually.

Elijah, a prophet from Gilead, had confronted Ahab with God's message. Ahab with his wife Jezebel had built a temple for Baal. Elijah warns them that because of this there will be years of severe drought. Not even dew will form. Elijah is courageous in his confrontation on behalf of God. He is full of faith with no hesitation to speak for the Lord. But instead of continuing in this strength, God tells Elijah to go hide himself at the brook of Cherith, east of the Jordan (1 Kgs 17:3).

Erosion

Colin Smith, senior pastor of The Orchard Evangelical Free Church in Illinois, explains the Cherith experience coming to every Christian at some point in their journey. He asks, "Why did God hide Elijah? Was it protection? Maybe, but God was able to protect Elijah when he marched into Ahab's palace. God protected him on Mount Carmel in the presence of all the prophets of Baal. So God did not need to send Elijah to Cherith to protect him. Was it a judgment on the people? Undoubtedly, yes. One way that God judges a nation is that he withdraws his teachers of the word of God. God hides his servants and there is a famine of the word."[1]

There was also another, deeper work accomplished in the chambers of Elijah's heart as his trust in the Lord expanded. "Cherith is the place where God withholds what you wanted most," Colin explains. "Cherith is the place where God closes the door on what you wanted to do for Him." Elijah had been prepared for a ministry as a prophet. His entire calling is to bring the word of God to the people. Instead he is sent into hiding in Cherith. There is no opportunity for him to use the gift.

"God can take you to Cherith by removing you from a position," Colin says. "God can take you to Cherith through a prolonged sickness that limits what you are able to do. Cherith is the place where God hides you and holds back what you most want to do." The pattern is all through Scripture, he points out. God hid Joseph in a prison before he came to the palace. He hid Moses in the desert for a third of his life before he led the people out of Egypt. God hid David in the mountains, running in and out of caves from Saul, before he was recognized as king. In the New Testament, God hid Paul for three years in Arabia after his conversion before he became a missionary. God hides Elijah at Cherith before his spectacular display of the living God at Carmel.

Elijah first spends time isolated at Cherith being cared for in a way comparable to the Israelites being provided manna in the desert. The ravens brought him bread and meat in the morning and bread and meat in the evening, and he would drink from the brook (1 Kgs 17:6). "And God will sustain you even at Cherith,"

---

1. Smith, "When God Hides You."

Colin says. The hinge is on Elijah's obedience. "So he went and did according to the word of the Lord" (v. 5). He had to have a time of being more deeply and entirely dependent on finding everything he needed from the Lord. This is a man of profound faith who was taken aside for the Lord to form within him an absolute knowing. When the brook dried up, Elijah again did according to the word of the Lord and traveled to a widow living in the town Zarephath until it was time to announce the end of the drought, not because there had been repentance but because the Lord would reveal himself again.

God spoke to Elijah to send him to assemble the false prophets on Carmel. He took twelve stones, one for each of the tribes of Israel, and built an altar in the name of the Lord. He placed the stones in a circle in the way the heads of each tribe stood with Joshua after they had crossed the River Jordan into the land of Israel (Josh 4:1–11). He dug a trench around it, arranged wood, cut the bull offerings into pieces and laid it on the wood. He had water drench the entire altar and fill the trench. Then the fire of the Lord ignited and came down and burned up the sacrifice, wood, stones, soil, and the water in the trench. When all the people saw this, they fell prostrate and cried, "The Lord, he is God!" Elijah commanded the 450 false prophets of Baal to be seized and killed, then went off to climb to the top of Carmel.

When Jezebel heard of this, she sent a message to Elijah threatening to have him killed. Elijah runs in fear. He comes to a bush and collapses under it. He asks God to let him die. He has had enough. He falls asleep and is awakened by an angel ministering food and nourishment for him. Strengthened, he traveled forty days and forty nights until he reached Horeb, the mountain of God where the law was given to Israel.

Generations before, God first appeared to Moses in a burning bush on Mount Horeb. As Moses approached the bush God told him not to come any closer, but to take off his shoes for he was on holy ground. When Moses returns to Horeb, he brings all the people of Israel to meet with God and receive the Ten Commandments. It is not just a burning bush. It is the entire mountain engulfed in fire and smoke (Exod 19:16–17). It is a place of drawing inward to receive direction for the confidence that is our strength. There Elijah went into a cave and spent the night (1 Kgs 19:2–9). The Lord sent a wind that shattered the rocks, an earthquake, fire, then stillness. These gave Elijah a picture of the destinies of man, in the form of the wind that erodes the foundation of the world we stand upon and disappears after a storm of death that makes man tremble, the fire of judgment, and the stillness that comes when the seventh seal is opened in heaven (Rev 8:1). It was when the quietness came over his soul that Elijah heard the Lord's gentle voice speak into his heart.

Elijah was summoned to a place where God had revealed himself to Moses as merciful and caring. Elijah had appeared as Israel's accuser, defending God's way. Now he is brought into the fortress of the Lord's mercy. He pulled his cloak over his face and went out to stand in the entrance of the cave. God asked what he is doing there. Elijah tells the Lord he feels he is the only one left who is loyal to God's covenant and now the people are trying to kill him too. But while Jezebel was killing off the Lord's prophets, Obadiah is remembered for hiding a hundred prophets in two caves, fifty in each. The Lord told him he had reserved seven thousand in Israel who had not bowed down to Baal. The Lord instructed Elijah to continue on to the desert of Damascus. He brings him renewed strength in the companionship of Elisha, who will walk with him (1 Kgs 18:10–19; 19:1–18).

It comes in a trickle, a drizzle of notes soft as water that carve out caves large and deep enough to shelter God's prophets. Every drop of God's word, even when not detected, makes an impression on the heart with unparalleled power to bring inner change. Story by story, sweeping the Earth, it has illuminated hundreds of thousands of lives to know the Lord. Challenging, comforting, inspiring, enlightening, contributing to collective understanding, every steady drop is the Lord's artistic ability to transform a space deepened with the renaissance of holiness.

Words that refine our torment into praise came one day at a time for Elijah and the widow in Zarephath. God had directed

Elijah to go to her, but when he arrived the widow told him she had no bread, only a handful of flour and a little oil. She was preparing herself and her son to die. Elijah said to her, "Don't be afraid." He instructed her to make the food. She did as Elijah had told her and there was food every day. The jar of flour was not used up and the jug of oil did not run dry. It was one small promise, "thus says the Lord," that attached her to God through the drought and famine. Abraham built his life on one promise: "so shall your descendants be." It was one word spoken to Peter, "come," and all of life in the Spirit opened for Peter. God had said to Elijah "go to this town" as he prepared the widow to be ready for his arrival (1 Kgs 17:7–16).

The blessing renewed each day. Elijah did not bring her a two-year supply of flour and oil. Her trust would have been placed in the supply, not in God who gave the supply. The ravens came to Elijah with just enough food for the day. "Give us this day our daily bread" (Matt 6:11). Whoever receives the one God sends receives Jesus. Whoever receives a prophet sent from God will get a prophet's reward (Matt 10:41). The widow received the same bread and food that Elijah received because she had responded to a simple message.

Christianity began within this inner hiddenness, suddenly knowing we are seen. We are understood. Faith moves within, steadily creating an inner sanctum that takes each of us into the expanse of God's restfulness. The trickle of words becomes a symphony of wonderment expressed in praise. Because of "the holy dwelling places of the Most High," "we will not fear, though the earth should change and though the mountains slip into the heart of the sea; though its waters roar and foam, though the mountains quake at its swelling pride" (Ps 46:2–4).

When Elijah called to God to send fire from heaven to consume the sacrifice, he prayed, "Answer me, Lord, answer me, so these people will know that you, Lord, are God, and that you are turning their hearts back again" (1 Kgs 18:37). Elijah is esteemed for being set apart to wait to be empowered in closer relationship with God's desires. Proverbs says, "The crucible is for silver and the furnace for gold, and each is tested by the praise accorded him"

(27:21). As a container, a crucible is used to hold precious metals when it is placed into a furnace to melt metals into its molten form and separate the dross so the impurities can be removed. Melted, silver and gold can be poured into a mold. The more purified the silver and gold, the more praise they receive for being precious.

A man is "tested by the praise accorded him." A crucible is a severe test to refine a person's character. When people speak about others and give them praise, they reveal someone's reputation based on external achievements or natural talents. The internal qualities of kindness, generosity, and honesty are of value to the Lord, who searches the heart, and should be what we praise in others. How we praise, whether with gratitude and genuine appreciation or with a critical spirit as we interact with others, also flows from what is tested in the heart. What we feel praise for reveals what is important to us. It may be for a way of making more material wealth, appearances, and gains in career. Or we may praise people who seek the Lord and grow in wisdom salted to strengthen others.

Moses' sister Miriam took a tambourine in her hand and all the women followed her with tambourines and dances after the people had crossed the Red Sea. She called to them to "Sing to the Lord, for He is highly exalted" (Exod 15:1–21). In contrast, when the men were returning home after David had killed the Philistine, the women came out from all the towns of Israel with singing and dancing, with joyful songs and with timbrels and lyres. As they danced they sang, "Saul has slain his thousands, and David his tens of thousands" (1 Sam 18:7). Glory for the victory was not given to God but to a human. The result was to anger Saul and make him fearful of losing the kingdom to David. The next day an evil spirit came into Saul and he picked up a spear and hurled it at David in an attempt to kill him (vv. 6–11). The kingdom disintegrated into bitter divisions.

Glory belongs to the Lord. The prophet Nathan assured David that God had declared the kingship would endure forever (2 Sam 7:16). This was forged with a covenant of salt (2 Chr 13:5). God named Aaron and his descendants as the priesthood of Israel with an everlasting covenant of salt (Num 18:19). Every sacrifice offered in the temple was to be salted (Lev 2:13). When God divided the upper waters and the lower waters on the second day of creation, the Midrash explains that the lower waters felt having to be in the lower spheres was farther from God and the heavens.[2] God then decreed that the water on Earth would be offered in the temple in the form of salt placed on every sacrifice. When water evaporates to heaven, salt stays in the physical realm, serving God to lift others to great heights.

The attendant blessing of being salt of the Earth is to influence with awareness, knowledge, and light. Salt flows downward from rivers, carrying ions of weathered rocks. It can flow upward from salt mines formed when the ocean covered the land, then covered the salt with shale or limestone to preserve the salt. Salt is a great absorber of heat when the dark gloom threatens to combust faith. Salt does not burn but will smother consuming fires.

Minerals that create rocks are made of crystals that form from salty water. In water, sodium and chlorine are separated. As the water evaporates the ions begin to bond together, forming crystals. A rock composed mostly of halite, called rock salt, is sedimentary rock. Halite does not become magma because large quantities of salt do not usually get buried deep enough to reach metamorphic pressures and hot temperatures. Halite is found where ocean water and salt lakes evaporate. The Dead Sea between Jordan and Israel has given enormous salt deposits thousands of feet thick as seawater evaporates.

Salt also weathers rocks by entering the cracks. The water evaporates and the salt builds up, pressuring rocks to split. Erosion moves the rock fragments and particles from land, carried by rivers into the process of changing. The salt is highly concentrated in the limestone and dolomite that built Jerusalem. The sodium is essential for life, for nerves and muscles to function and water to be allocated in the body. Its quantities on the ocean surface determine the cycles of rain. Its use by Jesus in calling us to be salt of the Earth (Matt 5:13) is a call to be men and women of character. Having salt

2. Rosenfeld, "Covenant of Salt."

within us is to cleanse an environment by bringing the influence of peace, as Israel did when they took possession of Canaan and rid the land of its pagan gods.

As Solomon wrote, "There is nothing new under the sun" (Eccl 1:9). It's not the horrors of the Holocaust or the Egyptian exile in today's world, but God's people are still struggling and their enemies continue to campaign against them. Miriam's life is a model of understanding that the harshest suffering precedes the redemption, in the dark hours before dawn lights the world. She knew that her people couldn't allow Pharaoh to break their spirit because she discerned that the time of the Lord's redemption had come. She had a penetrating sense of their future. When the people left Egypt they were so hurried they had no time for bread to rise. Yet Miriam took time to pack her tambourine. She was prepared for leading the women in dance and song in praise of the Lord. It is a song ready to stand up for beleaguered followers of Jesus in responsibility for the next generation to be filled with the music of Miriam.

The new song being written in our souls carries a melody we don't yet know, when all suffering and ignorance will be completely gone. It will be our ultimate song, containing all the joy of creation freed to be singing. It will be sung by those joined together who sought the Lord to be restored to God. Even Moses, whom God called his friend, needed the peacemaking skills of Aaron, the encouragement of Miriam, and the support of the seventy elders. We each will make a difference if we allow God the time to work his presence into our trust and discover there are angels in the depths of our valleys.

Moses began alone with God at the burning bush by saying, "I am not a man of words. I am heavy of speech and tongue" (Exod 4:10). By the time we reach his speeches in Deuteronomy delivered to Israel on the plains of Moab, Moses has become an eloquent prophet. God chose a man who was not a man of words, and when he spoke the people knew it was God who was speaking through him. Moses was humble, having an immense space within his heart where the Lord dwelt. The inner quiet propelled him to achieve the highest purpose of life by allowing God's blessing to come through him for his people.

"Not to us, O Lord, not to us, but to Your name give glory" (Ps 115:1).

7

Compression

Then the king commanded, and they quarried great stones, costly stones, to lay the foundation of the house with cut stones. (1 Kgs 5:17)

ROCKS ON EARTH'S SURFACE are unstable as the atmosphere weathers and erodes them into smaller fragments that are carried away, accumulating in layers given from streams, lakes, the sea, and air. The fragments are cached beneath dirt, rock particles and minerals mixing and cementing together. Often there are fossils in them when plants and animals are buried into the layers and turned into part of the stone.

To create rock from the many grains, minerals that form during burial and sedimentation adhere to the grains and precipitate minerals into spaces between the grains to hold them together. The most common cementing materials are silica and calcium carbonate, in an array of colors from clear quartz to amber feldspar and purples and reds from iron oxide.

This is where God meets life. The utter crushing is met with spectacular new events as he meshes heaven's knowledge with our inner desires. Gifts distill into tangible life as he melds a diversity into purpose within his body, fulfilling his prayer for us to be in oneness. Matthew 4:18–22 relates that Andrew and Peter were fishing, plying their trad, when called. The first thing Andrew did was to find his brother Simon and tell him, "We have found the Messiah" (John 1:35-42). Simon was known as the Zealot, active in politics and attempting to overthrow the Roman government. When he joined the others, his zealous spirit aligned with Jesus. As Jesus was leaving for Galilee, he called Philip to follow him. Philip found Nathanael and told him, "We have found the one Moses wrote about in the Law, and about whom the prophets also wrote—Jesus of Nazareth, the son of Joseph" (John 1:43-45). James and John were mending nets with their father. These two men were business owners along with their father and employed others in the business. Matthew, a tax collector, brought connections to the community and funding resources. Luke came from Antioch in Syria, a doctor skilled at research and keeping records. It was to Luke that Mary, mother of Jesus, confided what she'd kept in her heart.

The Lord brings gifts together and sends us into deeper waters, asking us, "where is your faith placed?" (Luke 8:25). Under great pressure, Paul did not want us unaware of the struggle, "burdened excessively, beyond our strength, so that we despaired even of life; indeed, we had the sentence of death within ourselves" (2 Cor 1:8). Just as during the four decades leading through the wilderness, God was working in the people to exercise their reliance on him, strengthen their sight of him, and persuade them of their own inadequacy and need of saving. When the weight of despair is so unendurable that we cannot bear even staying in this world, we've been freed to directly say to God, "I cannot do this. I need your help."

God acknowledges our fears more than three hundred times in his word. "Do not be afraid," he says to his people. It was Jesus' most repeated command. "Fear not." Feeling the power of fear, David was in anguish when he wrote Psalm 55. Distraught, terrorized, overwhelmed by the horrors of the enemy prowling the city with lies and violence, he calls upon God, wanting to connect with the infinite. "The Lord will save me," he writes, knowing it to be the only way he will fulfill his purpose on Earth.

Compression

Seeing the storms of wind and tossing waves, fear caused Peter to take his eyes off of Jesus. The loss of life, money, and resources or the anxiety of status can bring dread of hope grinding into dust. God tells us not to allow concerns to make us doubt his provision, his presence to keep us standing, or his power to fulfill his plan. Look below the surface and see who rules the winds and waves. Call out to him. He will come. David trusted God to do this. He wrote, "O fear the Lord, you His saints; for to those who fear Him there is no want" (Ps 34:9). When we are filled with awe of God, there is nothing else to fear. What can mere man do?

The confidence comes inseparable from humility because the humble person knows there is no limit to what God can accomplish. The uniqueness of those called out, their isolation, their resilience, defies the greatest opposition the world will ever know. The pagan Balaam summarized all those included in God's covenant when he said of Israel, "From the peaks of rocks I see them, from the heights I gaze upon them. This is a people who dwell alone not reckoning themselves one of the nations" (Num 23:9). The divine utterance of Ezekiel twenty-six centuries ago speaks to those who try to assimilate or dilute God's ordinances to fit more comfortably into a blind and deafened world: "You say, 'We want to be like the nations, like the peoples of the world, who serve wood and stone.' But what you have in mind will never happen" (Ezek 20:32).

At times it seems we have inherited a burden of having to live up to the heritage of spiritual heroes. An overwhelming volume of stories soaked in blood by martyrs for the Lord precedes us. We are possessors of a magnificent heritage. Believers find themselves struggling to uphold the tradition under layers of sediment, stacking up weight, pressuring the deepest layers to compact. It seems the sky is falling as Jesus creates beautiful stones. The path crumbles as he breaks down rocks and sets them afloat down a river. High mountain ranges are brought low by the forces of erosion, wearing them into piles of sediment. Thousands of years of building and plates colliding bring them up into high cliffs that witness to God's story.

The Rock from Which You Were Hewn

It was up Mount Moriah that Abraham, determined to keep faith, walked with his beloved son Isaac when the Lord called him to offer Isaac as a sacrifice. Wind, rain, the roots of trees, and burrows of animals had cracked parts of the stone of the mountain. Abraham and Isaac collected these stones to build an altar. An angel was sent here to stop Abraham from offering his son because God himself provided the sacrifice. A thousand years later, after the children of Israel received the commandments at the trembling mountain, wandered in the desert, and lived in the land for four hundred years under the judges, David became king. He purchased the land where Abraham brought Isaac and Jacob dreamt of a ladder ascending to heaven. David made Jerusalem his kingdom's capital. Canaanite people had cut stones out of the rock on the side of Mount Moriah to build walls and homes. The holes left from quarrying filled as cisterns for water.

The people were to increase the presence of light that resides in the world. God instructed, "You shall be holy" (Lev 19:2). God had breathed life into man, giving something of himself, spiritual and transcendent, to do God's work and illuminate beyond the superficial. Man was transformed from dust into a life that can seek out excellence. Our souls can perceive holiness and take on the goal to infuse our physical world with holiness, saying a blessing before eating, sanctifying marital relations, creating a space in time for worship, reflecting God's ideals, perceiving another's feelings, offering encouragement, and correcting wrong leanings. Which is why we are disturbed when someone professing faith cheats at business or behaves wrongly. It distances people from beauty and demoralizes community. It dims the light that has power within to break through to heaven and bring someone with us. Grace showers with the kindnesses but we still must be refined to implement the wisdom, restrain unbounded emotions, and acquire understanding to apply to the way we are to live.

In the darkest time of night the disciples were in a boat out on a lake. Jesus had sent them ahead of him to Bethsaida. The wind was strong and they were straining at the oars. During the last storm they were in Jesus was asleep in the boat, but now he is not with them. He was up on a mountain praying. But he saw them struggling in the lashing storm. He waited until just before dawn and went to them, walking on the lake. When they saw him they were terrified because they thought he was a spirit. Immediately Jesus spoke to them, "Take courage! It is I. Don't be afraid" (Matt 14:27). When he stepped into the boat with them, he gave them rest.

The disciples were amazed. Even though Jesus fed five thousand with five loaves of bread and two fish (Matt 14:13–21) and fed four thousand with seven loaves of bread and a few small fish (Matt 15:29–38), they had not understood. Scripture says their hearts were still hardened (Mark 6:45–52). Their thoughts may have fixed on Elisha, who, for more than six decades, stood as a prophet renowned for easing suffering. When a man came from Mount Ephraim bringing bread, barley loaves, and ears of corn, Elisha said to his attendant, "Give it to all the people gathered here." There were two thousand of his disciples there. One loaf would not feed hundreds of men. Elisha insisted. "Give it to them. For this is the word of God. They will eat and leave thereof." They all ate and had enough with bread left over (2 Kgs 4:42–44).

We can be that close to the wonders Jesus is doing and still not entirely receive all he offers. The world can plunge us in its deepest storm, into a situation of helplessness, and when our need is the greatest we learn that Jesus is willing to meet more than just our basic needs. His voice pierces the darkness. Don't be afraid. It is why we are told to count it all joy when we fall into trials. Our ascent to God is perfected under the pressures and completed as he fills in the space where we had not yet known him or each other. The disciples discovered they could trust him even when they could not see him. He was still there praying, still working to purify and refine them with a higher purpose than just rescuing them from that night.

The anguish when a son is sent to war, a woman wakes up without her husband beside her, or an elder sits alone waiting for death is in the desperate who look to Jesus because no one else can help. Time passes and continued disappointments cause us to ask,

"Why am I not enough?" Jesus understands loneliness so shattering even he cried out "Why? Why has the Father forsaken me?" He saw man's loneliness of soul and said it is not good for man to be alone. He brought each soul into community, and bestowed friendships brought with the fragrance of Jesus, a branch of a sheltering tree that protects from what is not his best plan for us. Yet with all this, we miss moments others need our response.

The day Jesus and his disciples were leaving Jericho, a large crowd followed him. Two blind men sitting by the road heard that Jesus was walking by. When they cried to him, "Lord have mercy on us, Son of David," the crowd told them to be quiet. So consumed were they with their own agenda, they had no patience to listen to someone on the fringe crying. Jesus turned and called to the blind men, asking "What do you want me to do for you?" They wanted their eyes to be open. Moved with compassion, Jesus touched their eyes and restored their sight. The two men followed him (Matt 9:27–31). He changed weapons of swords used for confrontation into the sword of his words responding to their cry.

No one came to Paul's defense, yet he said, "The Lord stood at my side and gave me strength" (2 Tim 4:17). When he speaks of contentment in Jesus, his mind is settled to rest on the power of the Lord and the beauty of heaven. He knows that only when we are walking with him according to his will can we have that peace. Society expects us to be stoic and have strength to push against the sediments weighing us down. But the coming of Jesus relieves us so we can be free to admit our weakness. It is honoring of God to be able to cry freely. He sends his Spirit and Paul discovers the confidence with clarity about who he is, a name written in heaven. He wants others to know who they are in God. He writes to Timothy, beloved as a son to him, as he is about to die and shares the encouragement in what he has learned. Paul did not identify himself as a defeated prisoner of a man. Though the world may have looked on him as having lost all that is worthwhile, Paul's last words to us are to say he has no cause to be ashamed. "There is laid up for me the crown of righteousness, which the Lord, the righteous Judge, will award to me on that day; and not only to me, but also to all who have loved His appearing" (2 Tim 4:8).

In their writings, the disciples never dwell on what they have given up to follow Jesus. Paul says he counts it as trash compared to knowing God's Son. He knows the outward man perishes and the inward man renews each day. Seeing eternal life offered instead of the eternity of darkness, they left their busy lives and put aside their own agendas. "Join with me in suffering for the gospel according to the power of God, who has saved us and called us with a holy calling" (2 Tim 1:8-9).

The world will never be a place of safety as we wait longingly for the Messiah's return. We will never achieve wholeness in this life because of the many parts of the world that remain separated from God. There are times of being in thick darkness, buried under on every side. Jesus sees us. He comes as light. Whoever follows the light will see the way forward. If we don't, we will be left in darkness as he passes by, water rushing past a stone. "You will die in your sin unless you believe" (John 8:24).

God says, "I will make a new covenant with you and remember your sins no more" (Heb 8:12; Rom 11:27; Jer 31:31-34; Heb 13:20). But we do not forget the stain we've created from our mistakes. It is difficult to absolve ourselves as remembering condemns us. His love cleanses of all unrighteousness and restores our heart. Yet our conscience is burdened by the thoughts of what we should have done differently. Some thorns remain needing to always be brought before Jesus and placed in our future in the time when he will reconcile all mistakes and wipe away all tears. The Lord does not want us to withdraw and hide our shame. He looks on the intent within our heart, not on our failures, refusing to allow yesterday's mistakes to prevent the fulfillment of our knowledge of him. When guilt weights us the world surrounds us with accusations, but when the error is brought to the Lord he will not condemn us.

As the nation was poised to enter the land of Israel, the Bible recounts forty years of their travels in the desert (Num 33:1). At some stages of the journey the people failed to believe God or failed to worship him alone. They made mistakes. Those who chose to have heaven's manna every day were indwelt with great endurance and they kept going, picking up after stumbling, wanting God. Speaking to his people when they were still slaves, God had handed them a promise to provide dignity and significance and gave manna to fulfill the way. He had told their father Abraham that they would be a great nation and in them all the families of the Earth would be blessed (Gen 12:2–3). He gives his words to hold onto as we enter the difficult phases, emphasizing that what's important is to turn to him and keep striving to reach beyond the horizon. We gain the ability to look upon our failures as the soul's motivation to glow brighter, wondering about the possibilities if we believe what the Lord says about our redemption. He created a world where hope is never lost because it is embedded from heaven's eternal light. Beyond all question, the mystery from which true godliness springs is great (1 Tim 3:16).

Asaph, one of the chief musicians of worship for the tribe of Levi during the reign of King David, penned Psalm 73, disclosing a time he came close to stumbling. "My steps had almost slipped. For I was envious of the arrogant as I saw the prosperity of the wicked." People in society "set their mouth against the heavens and their tongue parades through the earth." He was troubled. "I was senseless and ignorant," until he came into the sanctuary of God and perceived the truth. Trespassers outside of God's ways will end their days by being cast down to destruction and swept away by sudden terrors.

Asaph's heart was embittered by the easy life people seemed to live ignoring God. But "you have taken hold of my right hand. With your counsel you will guide me and afterward receive me to glory." Despite surrounding circumstance, he chooses to know God. "Whom have I in heaven but you?" Asaph says his stumbling would have betrayed the generation of God's children. He was aware of the serious responsibility to be an example of reverencing God in word and deed. So serious a command is it that it influences others around us. When Moses lost all patience and struck the rock in anger, "the Lord said to Moses and Aaron, 'Because

Compression

you have not believed Me, to treat Me as holy in the sight of the sons of Israel, therefore you shall not bring this assembly into the land which I have given them'" (Num 20:12). Upon this rock Jesus builds his church.

We come to each other in broken pieces with all sharp edges. Elijah came to Zarephath to a widow whose life had become meaningless. She walks into her son's room and finds he has died. Her human nature lets out the pain by blaming Elijah. So she says to Elijah, "What do I have to do with you, O man of God? You have come to me to bring my iniquity to remembrance and to put my son to death!" She is devastated by guilt, thinking her loss is a punishment for not measuring up to God's holiness. Elijah responds by listening to her anger against him. He says simply, "Give me your son." He does not try to reason with her anger. He asks her to put her heartache into his arms and share the anguish. Elijah carries the boy upstairs and brings it all to the Lord. Then he watches life come back into the son's body and his soul be restored to him. He comes down from the room and gives the boy to the grieving mother. "See, your son is alive" changes her tears into joy because now she has seen what the Lord is willing to do for her (1 Kgs 17:17–24). "I have heard of You by the hearing of the ear; but now my eye sees You" (Job 42:5).

The days under spiritual darkness bring opportunity to carry light to give sight of the Lord. Elijah gave kindness when kindness was not sought. When he led the enemy into Samaria after they were struck blind, the king of Israel asked if they should be killed. Elijah said no. "Set food and water before them so that they may eat and drink," and then he sent them home (2 Kgs 6:18–23). His kindness was sourced from seeing the army of angels sent from heaven, aware that the holiness of God is present.

Experiences against us do not define us but, like minerals, bind together to make memories with the Lord embedded in the new name on the white stone. All we've been forgiven will be in the white stone he bestows because even in the confusion God gave us a willingness to stand. Paul wrote, "Oh, the depth of the riches of the wisdom and knowledge of God! How unsearchable are his judgments, and unfathomable his ways! Who has known the mind of the Lord?" (Rom 11:33). He is beyond searching out. He wraps himself in light. He rides upon the storms and waters the mountains from his chambers. He looks at the Earth and it trembles. He touches the mountains and they smoke. We cannot see what he is doing in places so vast and deep only the Lord's voice can be heard.

"Have I not commanded you? Be strong and courageous! Do not tremble or be dismayed, for the Lord your God is with you wherever you go" (Josh 1:9).

8

Layered

There will not be left one stone upon another
which will not be torn down. (Luke 21:6)

STONES BEGIN AS MAGMA deep below the surface, bubbling up through the crust. It cools and becomes igneous rock. The years send wind, water, and gravity to weather it away. Rivers and wind carry it off in currents that slow and drop the particles on the bottom of the water and valleys and hills. The years deposit layer upon layer to build it up.

The land of Israel brims with layers. There are layers of history, roads, epic stories of faith, layers of the songs of people, politics, strife, and joy. Jerusalem is a story layered in stone built on beds a hundred feet beneath its surface. The hills ascend from pink and white chalk and grey misse stone that overlay thick strata of limestone embedded with flint and fossils. Hills of limestone slope beneath the Mount of Olives, where groves of trees provide the oil used to anoint kings and priests.

The mount rises east of Jerusalem, separating the holy city from the Judean desert's steep descent to the Dead Sea. King David left the city in despair and went barefoot up the Mount of Olives to escape from his son Absalom, who was conspiring against him

(2 Sam 15:30). After the destruction of the first temple, the Israelites began going there on pilgrimage because the glory of God had risen from Jerusalem and stood upon the mountain to its east (Ezek 11:23). During the time of the second temple, bonfires burned in rows of lights along the heights of the mount to carry the announcement of new moons to the Jews miles away in the diaspora.

Jesus enjoyed walking up on the hilltop and teaching there, where breathtaking views looked upon Jerusalem. He slipped off to pray alone on the hills to pour out his heart to the Father. Luke recorded Jesus' frequent visits to the Mount of Olives, where he went to pass the night and could gaze at the worlds of galaxies he had created. The mount holds memories of Jesus teaching the Lord's Prayer, weeping over Jerusalem, and his ascension, when angels accompanied him from the summit of the mount into heaven. Two angels spoke to the disciples on the Mount of Olives to tell them Jesus will return in the same way they had seen him go into heaven (Acts 1:11). Zechariah prophesied, "In that day His feet will stand on the Mount of Olives, which is in front of Jerusalem on the east; and the Mount of Olives will be split in its middle from east to west by a very large valley, so that half of the mountain will move toward the north and the other half toward the south" (Zech 14:4). An earthquake splitting along the fault lines in the rocks creates a passage for the people to escape through the mountains, much as the people escaped Pharaoh through the Red Sea.

Life itself began to make rocks to layer the strata for the triumphs God desires. From the oldest marine animal found, the trilobites that scurried on the ocean floor, the thick shells of calcium carbonate are the mineral composing Jerusalem's limestone. God distilled the elements for the mountains and for Jerusalem's walls and the layers of architecture, governments, and conversations that built its future. The stone is multicolored in shades of white, beige, and pink, called Jerusalem of Gold because of its glow from the setting sun. The ancient stone distinguishes the city from all others in the world.

Layered

For three thousand years the holy city of Jerusalem has been destroyed, rebuilt, taken apart, and built again with the stone laying beneath the mountains. The sixteen-hundred-foot-long wall on the western side of the temple mount is forty-five layers of limestone. Twenty-eight of the layers are above ground. Seventeen layers of the Western Wall's stones are unseen underground, part of the foundation built on a hill. Each stone of the first seven layers above ground is enormous, weighing up to seven tons. On top of these stones are layers from the Romans, the Crusaders, and the Ottomans. Each cut the stones in different ways and laid them in different patterns, some smoothed and some left raw. The highest layers include smaller stones from the thirteenth to the sixteenth centuries, many from the lower layers, picked up and used again. The largest building stone found in Israel is in the tunnel under the temple mount—44.6 feet long, 10.8 feet deep, and weighing 570 tons. The massive stones stabilize the wall, withstanding the disaster of earthquakes.

The psalmist sang about the stone that the builders would reject becoming the chief corner stone (118:22). The stones of Jerusalem's ancient temple were built for a place to meet with God, the cornerstone of wisdom and peace among the nations. The destruction of the temple is mourned because our work is not yet completed. Feeling the loss of its presence stirs the heart to acts that bring something in the world back to God, restoring land to health, water to its pristine state, a friend's mind to hopeful expectation, nations to know the Lord. This is the prayer when hands reach to touch the broken places in the Western Wall. When the Messiah returns the stones of the holy city will usher in peace to rebuild all his people of the world. "At that time they will call Jerusalem 'The Throne of the Lord,' and all the nations will be gathered to it, to Jerusalem, for the name of the Lord; nor will they walk anymore after the stubbornness of their evil heart" (Jer 3:17).

Below ground the *meleke*, the royal layer, has been excavated to make hundreds of caverns, cisterns, and aqueducts that honeycomb the city of Jerusalem, percolating water for the citizens. Communities settled around the freshwater sources bringing a steady flow to Jerusalem, filtering and purifying through limestone. David built a palace here with stones from the layer of rock made by the dust of the tiny sea creatures. When freshly cut, *meleke* is pure white limestone, the stone of kings. It is soft and workable when quarried, then when exposed to sun and air it hardens with a clear surface that withstands nature's erosion.

The royal stone is the foundation of Jerusalem's stories. "You shall seek the Lord at the place which the Lord your God will choose from all your tribes, to establish His name there for His dwelling, and there you shall come" (Deut 12:5). God's prophetic mark was placed in Genesis 21 when he told Abraham he was to sacrifice Isaac on the mountain. Then, when a plague broke out in Israel during David's time and seventy thousand men died, an angel stretched out his hand toward Jerusalem to destroy it too. God stopped him, saying, "Enough! Now withdraw your hand." The angel of God was by the threshing floor of Araunah the Jebusite. David bought the threshing floor and built an altar to God there. He offered burnt offerings and fellowship offerings (2 Sam 24:15–25).

It was on this site the temple was built. The foundation stone is the holiest site on Earth, the junction of heaven and Earth. It is where Abraham prepared to sacrifice his son. The rock is located toward the center of the temple mount, a platform built and expanded over the centuries. It was where the holy of holies was during the time of the temple. The ark of the covenant was placed on the foundation stone inside the holy of holies during Solomon's temple. The ark was not present during the second temple and the stone was used by the high priest to offer incense and sacrifices during Yom Kippur.

The rock is part of the surrounding limestone. Its edge forms a ledge with a gap under it, where steps from the Dome of the Rock lead to the Well of Souls beneath, a stone cave inside the foundation stone. The foundation stone is where John the Baptist was announced to Zechariah as he was performing priestly responsibilities. The angel said, "Do not be afraid, Zacharias, for your petition has been heard, and your wife Elizabeth will bear you a son, and you will give him the name John . . . and he will be filled with the Holy Spirit while yet in his mother's womb. And he will turn many of the sons of Israel back to the Lord their God" (Luke 1:11–16).

The gospel story begins on this site with the difficulty to believe what seems too impossible. The story ends with unshaken knowledge of the hand of God willing to stop death from exacting punishment. John the Baptist told the people of Judea, "His winnowing fork is in His hand to thoroughly clear His threshing floor, and to gather the wheat into His barn; but He will burn up the chaff with unquenchable fire" (Luke 3:17). Sifting wheat from chaff reappears in the Last Supper when Jesus turned to Peter and said, "Simon, Simon, behold, Satan has demanded permission to sift you like wheat; but I have prayed for you, that your faith may not fail" (Luke 22:31–32). Grace upon grace from the story of the Lord flows into the world to gather his stones. He sat on the Mount of Olives and spoke to his followers about the ending of the story. "See to it that no one misleads you," he said. "See that you are not frightened" (Matt 24:3–5).

Hundreds of caverns, cisterns, tombs, and aqueducts have been provided by the stone God used to create the hills of Israel. Solomon drafted workers to quarry huge blocks to build the temple in the place Abraham had built an altar to God. He laid the foundation with hewn stone. The people came, a people who had been gathered from the mountain where God had spoken his commandments. They gave generously, investing the work of their own hands as Jacob did when he picked up stones to build his altar.

This work went quickly and prospered in their hands (Ezra 5:8). Inside the inner sanctuary a pair of cherubim carved from olive wood towered fifteen feet high with wings outstretched to touch the walls and each other's wings in the middle of the room (1 Kgs 6:23). Radiating the reminder that cherubim guard the way to the tree of life in the garden, where a choice was given to mankind, they symbolized God's presence always with us as we choose life each day.

When the temple was complete, Solomon prayed for all the peoples of Earth to know God's name as his people Israel did and recognize this house of prayer bears his name (1 Kgs 8:43). The people served God in the temple until the Babylonians destroyed it four hundred years later. The Israelites were expelled from the land. When they returned from exile to live surrounded by another culture the second temple was built. Herod employed laborers to cut enormous stones from the layers of rock to build a temple higher than fifteen stories from marble and gold. He had a plaza built around the temple, surrounded by walls on all four sides supported by rows or arches. Artisans were employed to create beautiful mosaics and frescos.

As Jesus was leaving the temple with Peter, James, and Andrew, one of them said to him, "Look, Teacher! What massive stones! What magnificent buildings!" As they sat on the Mount of Olives they looked at the splendor of the temple spread out over acres beneath God's sky, marveling at it and the decades of work that went into it. But Jesus said the stones of the temple would be thrown down. These were disturbing words. For the disciples, the center of their world was the temple, where they met with God (Mark 13:1–4). His presence was found at the place he chose in Zion (Deut 12:5). The temple represented unity. Nothing could be added to it or taken from it or the balance would be spoiled.

By summer 68 A.D. Romans had brutally slaughtered more than half a million Jews in Jerusalem, including visitors there to give thanks for Passover. Many scattered throughout other nations and many were shipped off to be forced into gladiator games. By year 73 Israel no longer celebrated God at the temple. Josephus recorded how the Romans torched the city and the temple with fires raging so hot the gold fittings melted and ran into the cracks between the stones. Fire still burned a month later.

The temple complex was a series of concentric circles of purity, each area limited to a more select group of people. There were two courts. One was for the Israelites only and the other, an outer court, was the court of the Gentiles, used by strangers from other nations. The two courts were separated by a low stone wall Josephus described as four and a half feet high with thirteen openings. When Paul spoke of the death and resurrection of Jesus breaking down the middle wall of partition that separated Jew and Gentile (Eph 2:14), he alludes to this dividing wall. Warning stones were placed along the top of the dividing wall, carved in Greek inscriptions marking the boundary where Gentiles could not enter the sacred places. A slab of this limestone, now fractured and chipped by age, sits on a shelf at the Israel Museum in Jerusalem. It is translated:

> No stranger is to enter within the balustrade round the temple and enclosure.
> Whoever is caught will be responsible to himself for his death, which will ensue.

The innermost place in the temple, the holy of holies, was only accessible to the high priest, and only on the holiest day of the year, the Day of Atonement. Jesus became the foundation, the cornerstone, our sanctuary where we meet with God and life can be restored. The ones who stand on this precious stone will not be ashamed (1 Pet 2:6). When buildings and the worlds around us are torn down, we will not be disturbed. We who take refuge have strong encouragement to enter behind the veil that once separated the holy of holies because Jesus has entered ahead of us, becoming high priest forever (Heb 6:18–20).

When he came into the world, he came into each nation to draw us into his kingdom. John saw no temple in the new holy city because the Lord God and Jesus are its temple. Having the glory of God, the new Jerusalem's brilliance will be like a costly stone. The street of the city will be pure gold, absorbing and reflecting the light shining on its surface. The foundation stones of the city's high wall are inlaid with precious stones—jasper, sapphire, agate, emerald, onyx, carnelian, chrysolite, beryl, topaz, chrysoprase, jacinth, and amethyst. The gems the Lord selected are all anisotropic stone, reflecting the colors of the rainbow when rays of pure light pass through and refract in different directions to illuminate the intensity of the minerals. And there was a rainbow around the throne, like an emerald in appearance (Rev 4:3). An angel stands at each of the twelve gates and the names of the twelve tribes of Israel are written on them. The gates are twelve pearls, brilliant with a glowing luster caused by light shining through its translucent layers and reflecting back from deep within the pearl (Rev 21:19–22, 26).

Knowing the sovereign God is greater than any beautiful building that man could construct, the Lord provided the final atonement that would transform the layers of our hearts into dwelling places for God's light to be illuminated. "Do you not know that you are a temple of God and that the Spirit of God dwells in you?" (1 Cor 3:16).

Our future is built on the layers of stories that prepared the way. In the shadow of Mount Moriah, bent and bleeding, Jesus walked 650 yards to Golgotha. He was weak and in shock. That morning Jesus had been whipped by balls of lead embedded in leather straps, brought down with full force to shred his shoulders and back. Mary looked up at her son dying on the cross. Thirty years before, holding Jesus in her arms after he was born, she and Joseph had brought him to the temple. Moved by the Spirit, Simeon, a man of faith, said to her, "And a sword will pierce your own soul too" (Luke 2:35).

She understood pain that comes from following God's will. She knew that her son had been born for a higher purpose, but she could see no victory in the bleeding child whom Simeon had said would be a light to the Gentiles and the glory of her people Israel (Luke 2:32). She confided in Luke that the angel Gabriel had come to her and told her she would have a son who would be a great man, the Son of God, and be given the throne of his ancestor David to be king of Israel forever. His kingdom would never end (Luke 1:31–35). "Don't be afraid, Mary," Gabriel had said to her. God had prepared her, forewarned her, but the sorrow in a mother's heart witnessing the torture and death of her child would not fully be replaced with the glory of God's purpose until she saw him risen from the dead and returned to his people.

With all his effort he pushed himself up to breathe the words, "It is finished." When he breathed his last breath and descended into death, all nations became bonded to the nation of Israel under God's covenant. On the third day Jesus rose triumphantly, bringing us all up with him. As his Spirit moves across the Earth, the layers of history that separate us dissolve as people from each nation are born anew to one Father. Layers that cover over us with shame, anger, blame, failures, betrayals, and the accuser of God's people are washed away and new layers of prayer rise, asking him to bring us more light.

Those rejoined to God don't know each other in the way people know each other in the world. A leper gives thanks with a tax collector. Susanna, who brought resources, worshipped with a former prostitute. There are no longer shadows that we look at to measure our differences. Instead each, doing the will of God as fully as they are empowered, directs their thoughts to see the image of God. There is no partiality (Jas 2:1). "Then I will know fully just as I also have been fully known" (1 Cor 13:12). The law of liberty given by the king assesses what the world cannot see. Knowing what makes each of us unique, he sees who loves to sing, who holds quiet hope in himself. He knows if friends depend on us, when we laugh, and how our unseen tears were never acknowledged. To him we are enough.

The Shema, the central prayer among Israelites, says, "Hear, O Israel: The Lord our God, the Lord is one" (Deut 6:4). It is a call for the nation to gather to God and a hope for the world to come to him too. "You shall have no other gods before me" (Exod 20:3). In the Shema the relief of certainty in his prophetic promise presses through the sadness of today's realities. With what joy Jesus went into Galilee proclaiming the hope to his people. "The time is fulfilled," he said, "and the kingdom of God is at hand; repent and believe in the gospel" (Mark 1:14–15).

He came down from heaven rejoicing for us. Seeking those who worship in the absolute truth of their hearts revealed by his Spirit, he gathers living stones to build his kingdom, a glory that will outlast all politics, doubters, shame, persecutions, shining to extinguish all lies. They are to repair the broken walls (Isa 58:12). As living stones we are a wall guarding the truth to give to others, boundaries along a narrow bridge that has a series of dangerous crossings. To navigate that narrow path we need to be brought into relationship with others in his body to mentor us across treacherous places we are not able to see. A person who will tell us when we are making a misstep and keep us from falling is someone who clarifies what the Lord wants us to understand.

"Thus says the Lord who made the earth, the Lord who formed it to establish it, the Lord is His name, 'Call to Me and I will answer you, and I will tell you great and mighty things, which you do not know'" (Jer 33:2-3).

METAMORPHIC

Morph Means to Change, Transformed

The earth, from it comes food, and underneath
it is turned up as fire. (Job 28:5)

9

Colliding

Therefore I have set my face like flint. (Isa 50:7)

FLINT IS A HARDENED knot of the mineral quartz occurring as glassy grey, black, green, white, or brown colors enclosed in sedimentary rocks such as chalks and limestone. It is thought that flint formed while sediments converted into rocks being weathered by waves in the chalk seas.[1] Over hundreds of years, skeletons from organisms such as sea sponges and diatoms scatter in the seabed and mix with the sediments, which decompose upward as oxygen diffuses downward from the water columns. Many different opaline shells, echinods, and worms burrow deeply into the sediments. After the organisms die the burrows fill with sediment. Flint forms from the crystalline particles within the old burrows into nodular shapes reflecting the living spaces.

Flint splits into thin, sharp blades when struck by a hard object to be used as tools, weapons, fire starters, and gems. The process is called knapping. "Make for yourself flint knives and circumcise again the sons of Israel the second time" (Josh 5:2). Because of uneven expansion and impurities, flint cannot be exposed to fire

1. Bone, "How Flint Is Formed."

or it tends to fracture into pieces. To prevent it from fragmenting, flint is heated slowly and slowly cooled to homogenize its elements and make it more knappable for cleaner, sharper edges.

When Isaiah penned prophetic words of faith he said, "The Lord God has given me the tongue of disciples, that I may know how to sustain the weary one with a word." He did not turn back, even giving his back to those who struck him, his cheeks to those who painfully plucked his beard, and his face to the humiliation of being spit on. "For the Lord God helps me . . . Therefore, I have set my face like flint" (Isa 50:7). Isaiah had walked a long time with the Lord to be tempered and taught his need of the Lord's strength to know what it meant to set his face like flint.

When God walked with his Son up to Jerusalem to the stake of execution for us, Jesus climbed the hills of fossiliferous limestone, flint, and chalk deposited by God's flood judgment of man's transgressions. After Jesus committed his spirit into the hands of his Father, death collided with Jesus, intolerance collided with holiness, and the Father announced himself in rocks splitting and the whole Earth quaking (Matt 27:51). The event was so significant that it echoed into heaven and the veil that separated the entrance to the holy of holies was torn from top to bottom. The veil was heavy, sixty feet high, thirty feet wide, and as thick as a handbreadth. The moment Jesus proclaimed, "It is finished!" the holy place where God's presence dwelt on the mercy seat was opened to those asking forgiveness through Jesus (Mark 15:37–38). The relationship between God and humanity was forever changed. The apostle Paul explained, "But now in Christ Jesus you who formerly were far off have been brought near by the blood of Christ" (Eph 2:13). The apostles walked this holy territory, becoming tempered like flint, committed even to dying so that we would know.

Metamorphosis caused by the earthquake shaking the land when Jesus died brings change from the depths within, allowing God to battle with us against a world influencing us to conform to its patterns. After Ezekiel absorbed the scroll of God's words, he too was sent to speak for God whether or not people listen or fail to listen. "Like emery harder than flint I have made your forehead.

COLLIDING

Do not be afraid of them or be dismayed before them, though they are a rebellious house" (Ezek 3:9).

Emery stone is an aggregate of minerals rich in corundum, which is exceptionally hard, the third hardest mineral after diamond and moissanite. Corundum is a rock-forming mineral found in igneous, sedimentary, and metamorphic rocks.[2] Sometimes it is found as beautiful transparent crystals in many different colors perfect for cutting into gemstones. A specimen of corundum with a deep red color is a ruby. If it has a blue color it is called sapphire. Colorless corundum is known as white sapphire. Corundum of any other color is known as fancy sapphire.

Diamonds are formed in metamorphic rocks. Limestone alters into marble. Clay and volcanic ash becomes slate, giving use for roofing tiles, electrical insulators, and as a whetstone to sharpen knives. The transformation is found where mountains build and tectonic plates shift, crushing rock caught between the collision or heated from hot magma below. The repeated opening and closing of ocean basins or new magma upwelling spreads ridges apart and the new rocks are carried through the fractures, altered and recrystallized to change their composition to hold precious gems.

Ideologies and cultures we perceive separating us are irrelevant when we are subjected to challenges within difficult times in which the Lord works changes. We are pressed together, becoming vessels of precious gems. We come to appreciate the struggle in each other. We recognize the grieving when tragedy occurs. We share the victory when the rocks quaked and Jesus rose from death.

When he died and the Earth darkened, the Chamber of Hewn Stones and its enormous thirty-foot-long stone lintel, weighing about thirty tons, cracked. The hall was the meeting place of the Sanhedrin during the days of the second temple. Built into the north wall of the temple, half inside the sanctuary and half outside, it had doors providing access to both the temple and the outside. The Sanhedrim was the high court of justice of the Jews, known as the *Concilium*, or grand council (Matt 26:59; Luke 22:66). At the time of Jesus seventy-one members were divided

2. King, "Corundum."

into three chambers—the chamber of the priests, the chamber of the scribes, and the chamber of the elders. Each was composed of twenty-three members, which together with the presidents numbered seventy-one.

The New Testament writers described these priests, the scribes, and the ancients assembled to judge Jesus (Mark 14:53; 16:1; Matt 15:21; John 11:47; Acts 4:5). Judging the Messiah was the last act that the Sanhedrin made from the temple. Possibly the damage from the earthquake caused them to move from the Chamber of Hewn Stones and meet elsewhere. The law no longer went forth from the temple.

To redeem the entire creation, Jesus was put on the cross in the morning. From noon until three in the afternoon darkness came over the whole land (Matt 27:45). Darkness is a frequent sign of judgment (Amos 5:18; 8:9). The ninth plague of the exodus was darkness over the land of Egypt for three days, a presence so thick that it was tangible (Exod 10:21–22). After the darkness came the death of the firstborn sons (Exod 11:4–5). Darkness preceded judgment. Isaiah beheld the Lord coming to lay land desolate and destroy sinners out of it, the sun darkened and the moon not causing her light to shine. Ezekiel foretold God covering the heaven, making the stars dark and covering the sun with a cloud. Jesus reminded the people, saying the sun will be darkened and the moon will not give light (Mark 13:24).

The sky darkening over the cross was a horrible condemnation, full of shame and fear, a cruel death, and yet it became the symbol of unsurpassed beauty lifted by divine light victoriously high over death and judgment. The angels long to look into this mystery. They watched from heaven when the Lord was born into humanity. They stayed with him at every step, still worshipping him (Heb 1:6; 1 Tim 3:16). Ministering to him, they spread a table for him after his forty-day fast, as they did for Elijah when he collapsed exhausted under a tree. An angel again stood with him when he entered into agony in Gethsemane.

The raging enemy death has lost its power. Even when we die, the gems we become remain in Jesus, mined from the dust. No part of our heart is lost. The soul and body, willing in life to give all to the Lord, are rejoined in him to become the body the Lord breathes life into to achieve its vitality as a human being in the new heaven and new Earth. Resurrection will bring wholeness of body and soul, which together are the image of God. The union with the source of all life is the ultimate achievement, a level of joy beyond our experience. As it is said, no eye has ever seen it (Isa 64:3).

The heavens roll back, the Earth trembles, and despairing souls encounter their Savior coming through the presence of darkness. He sees how suffering wounds the hearts of his people and he has made a way to lift them to heaven. We were dead in transgressions. We were unable to respond to God until he opened heaven and called to us. "He awakens my ear to listen as a disciple. The Lord God has opened my ear" (Isa 50:4–5). The power that creates life comes to the people walking in darkness. They see a great light shining on them (Isa 9:2).

When Paul was on the road to Damascus breathing threats against the Lord's disciples, particles of light from heaven suddenly flashed around him. The thundering light rocked him and the others with him to their knees, and Jesus, speaking in his Hebrew language, asks a piercing question. "Shaul, Shaul why do you persecute me?" (Acts 9:1–9; 22:7; 26:14). When the Lord called out, "Abraham! Abraham!" to stop him from sacrificing Isaac at the altar, Abraham replied, "Here I am" (Gen 22:11). Also calling his name twice, the Lord came to Samuel and called, "Samuel! Samuel!" Then Samuel said, "Speak, for your servant is listening" (1 Sam 3:10). To respond by saying "I'm listening" is a moment of being entirely at peace with yourself.

But Paul asks, "Who are you Lord?" At times we are not ready to say, "Here I am, I'm listening." Instead we are asking, "Who are you Lord? We want to see you. We want to understand." God cloaks himself so we feel our desire to be close to him. It's in our need that we find true strength and destiny, especially in the difficult experiences. We may feel God's face is concealed but if we could see his presence all the time, we would lose the opportunity to cultivate growth. He gives us freedom to choose him to bring out the greatest light. His people's stories rise from voids where there is no one else to support their struggle or guide their direction.

In response to wanting to know who he is, Jesus tells Paul to go into Damascus, where he will be taught. Paul had been blinded by heaven's bright light, later writing that the Lord "dwells in unapproachable light, whom no one has ever seen or can see" (1 Tim 6:16). Paul was brought out of the blindness so that he may know the truth of the resurrection and know Jesus with "participation in his sufferings, becoming like him in his death, and so, somehow, attaining to the resurrection from the dead" (Phil 3:10–11).

It is one thing to await the return of Jesus. It is another to be willing to follow him into a wilderness with an uncertain future. We like security. A decision to place ourselves in situations where we have to renew trust each day for provision is not an easy plan for survival. We think of manna as miraculous food provided for the Israelites to stave off starvation in the desert. But soon after the manna began coming down from heaven, the people received the Torah at Mount Sinai. For four decades they were given manna so that they could learn about God's ways. The only people in the world who were learning this relationship with God were those who absorbed the manna.

After the forty years, they crossed the Jordan River into the promised land. The manna stopped. God now gave them vineyards, fields, and orchards. Bread was harvested from the land and baked in ovens. God provides both the manna from heaven and the land that yields earthly food. The desert generation that recognized that both these blessings came from God was given the same responsibility given to us to accept manna so we are enabled to work the will of God on Earth. With it, suffering combines with joy, loss mixes with celebration and becomes a testament.

The Lord presides over boundaries laid between life and death, night and day. He placed the sand as the boundary for the sea, though waves toss they cannot prevail over it (Jer 5:22). He inscribed a circle on the surface of the waters at the boundary between light and darkness (Job 26:10). He made a boundary around the times and lands of every nation (Acts 17:26). He defines love with boundaries encasing his care. And he made us to live and move and have our being in him (Acts 17:28). Our hope is forward looking, directing steps toward receiving the Lord. Tribulation presses our focus toward the other side, knowing there are boundaries around darkness.

All rock can be heated. Any rock can become igneous if it is melted, cools, and hardens. Any rock can become sedimentary if it is broken by weathering and erosion and the pieces are bonded together in new combinations. Any rock can become metamorphic if it is exposed to intense pulsing heat and pressures pushing against it. We all are made of clay from the dust of the ground to be fashioned into a living temple.

When Isaiah heard the voice of the Lord and said to the Lord, "you are our potter and all of us are the work of your hand," he was giving himself to the Lord to make of his life whatever he chose, knowing he was made of the dust of the ground (Isa 64:8). The power of the Holy Spirit to touch a life is to hear something that is beyond the range of others to see. Paul was entirely dependent on the Lord and needed to be led. He fasted for three days as Esther did when she needed victory with the king. He met with Ananias, who laid hands on him, received the Holy Spirit, was baptized, and received by the disciples there (Acts 9:15–16, 19; 22:12–16). He would come to write of his confidence in Jesus to guard all that his faith placed in the hands of the Lord until the day all is restored (2 Tim 1:12).

God uses the darkness to bring to remembrance the gift of his light. To guide the people through the wilderness on the way to holy land, God revealed the design for the menorah to Moses on the mountain. The lampstand was made of pure gold with six branches and seven lamps. The priests kept the lamp of God burning from evening until morning in the tabernacle to light the space in front of it (Exod 25:31–40; 27:21). It was a response of profound awareness that the wilderness is not the end of the story. It was the remarkable act of the people to continue lighting lamps wherever they were scattered after the temple stones were dismantled.

As we are going in our lives, we have been given oil to bring appreciation of the light when the darkness encounters light. Revealing what is ahead of us, interlocking the focus on Jesus, we bring his light to those who are becoming God's gems through staggering changes. We will sing for joy over your victory (Ps 20:4–5). Bringing light to show that the darkest pain is understood draws others nearer to the beauty of the Lord, who makes life from the dust.

God spoke, "let there be light" (Gen 1:3). Jesus came saying, "I am the light" (John 8:12). Then Jesus said, "You are the light, a city on a hill" (Matt 5:14), strategically placed. The power that made all life lives in us.

10

Transformation

For no man can lay a foundation other than the one which is laid, which is Jesus Christ. (1 Cor 3:11)

SCORCHING HEAT AND THE persistent pressure of metamorphism form limestone and dolomite into marble, a word derived from the Greek *marmaros*, meaning "shining stone." Composed of minerals such as clay, micas, quartz, pyrite, iron oxides, graphite, and calcite, the sediments and rock fragments that create the beautiful marble are pressed into gleaming rock during compaction.

The calcite crystals in limestone are very small, a sugary sparkle in the light. As metamorphism progresses and applies more pressure, the crystals grow larger and stronger, turning the rock denser and harder as the calcite interlock with one another. As we are being built into a spiritual house (1 Pet 2:5), the Lord's word goes through the world shared by one person to the next, interlocking lives, filling the gullies left by channels of emptiness in our souls.

Rocks change other rocks. We form a bond based on others knowing we see them, aware of a struggle that is important to them. When Moses spoke of following God, the Israelites could not hear the message because of how despondent they had become under oppressive slavery. The Lord came alongside them, walked with them, cared for them, and a relationship developed so that they could hear the wonder of his plan. John the Baptist came and Jesus said of him he is the greatest of men who was born of women, before the new birth baptizing into the Lord's death and with the Holy Spirit. John's great work was to prepare a way for the people to hear the Lord (Luke 7:28). The church is to be cloaked in this kindness and bestowed with invitations to prepare the world to receive Jesus into every aspect of life (Eph 1:3–4).

Carefully carved to fit perfectly together in a culture cruelly telling each other "you're OK" instead of saying "you're under the wrath of God and he wants to bring you into his plan," the *ekklesia* is formed within the boundaries that define royal love. The apostle's letters are filled with messages for the collective church experience. Let us fear. Let us hold fast. Let us draw near (Heb 4). Emotional struggles bound them together under ill treatment, sharing resources to meet needs, and sheltering each other's individual journeys. Each has come having refined convictions, etched with forgiveness, chiseled with strata declaring triumph, each sculpted by the hand of God. The changes are forged within the hidden chambers of each heart, where the spirit of God intercedes for us with groaning too deep for words (Rom 8:26). Soren Kierkegaard stressed the private indwelling of belief in the knight of faith in his 1847 *Works of Love*:

> Consider the woman with hemorrhages; she did not press herself forward in order to touch Christ's robe; she told no one what she had in mind and what she believed she said very softly to herself, "If I only touch the hem of his robe, I shall be healed." The secret she kept to herself; it was the secret of faith that saved her both temporally and eternally. You can keep the secret to yourself also when you profess your faith with bold confidence, and when you lie weak on your sickbed and cannot move a limb when you cannot even move your tongue, you can still have the secret within you.[1]

---

1. Kierkegaard, *Works of Love*, 28–29.

Transformation

Being birthed from the rock of the Lord, the force of God's thunder is heard rolling in the hearts of the redeemed as they interlock under the pressure of troubles. We are all in this battle. Jesus was not dissatisfied with the Pharisees because they lacked knowledge. They were well studied in God's word. Paul was a Pharisee chosen by the Lord, highly skilled in handling the word. It was relationship that was missing. Day after day the people seek God and seem eager to know his ways, Isaiah declared. Their prayers were not answered. Truth stumbled in the street. The Lord offered remedy, saying to loose the chains of injustice, break the yoke, free the oppressed, share food with the hungry, shelter the poor wanderer, clothe the naked, and don't turn away from the needs of your own family. Then your light will break forth like the dawn (Isa 58:1–8).

"Have you not read what God said to you . . ." (Matt 22:31). Each time Jesus asked this question he made an important point about remembering the spiritual presence of God interacting with relationship. "Have you not read what David did when he became hungry, he and his companions?" (Matt 12:3). "Or have you not read in the Law, that on the Sabbath the priests in the temple break the Sabbath and are innocent?" (Matt 12:5). "Have you not even read this Scripture: 'The stone which the builders rejected, this became the chief corner stone'" (Mark 12:10). "Have you not read that He who created them from the beginning made them male and female?" (Matt 19:4).

The people were faulted for having let go of the commands of God and holding on to the traditions of men (Mark 7:8). The characteristics he is forging are not in terms of ritual observance but humane traits of mercy, modesty, and kindness. Prayers seeking reprieve most often carry regrets for dishonesty, deception, and unkindness toward others, not about traditions of men. He wanted his words to bind the people.

When Israel was about to enter their land, it was a new beginning. Before they crossed the Jordan, Moses and the elders charged them. "So it shall be on the day when you cross the Jordan to the land which the Lord your God gives you, that you shall set up for yourself large stones and coat them with lime and write on them all the words of this law, when you cross over, so that you may enter the land which the Lord your God gives you, a land flowing with milk and honey, as the Lord, the God of your fathers, promised you . . . You shall write on the stones all the words of this law very distinctly" (Deut 27:1-8).

Writing the words of God fixes the ideas in the mind of the writer. "Write them upon the tablet of your heart" (Prov 7:3). It was usual to write the text on parchment, the treated hide of an animal. But now God says, "This day you have become a people for the Lord your God" (v. 9), and the laws are to be inscribed on stone. The parchment suggests the outer part of a life, but the stone represents the unchangeable foundation life is built upon. Faith is fully sighted because the holy word attached them to heaven to influence the outer manifestation of being purified.

Recrystallization is what distinguishes highly valued marble. Recrystallization purifies the rock and obscures the fragments and sediments as it alters into solid shining marble. If metamorphosis is incomplete, marble retains impurities such as iron oxides, remaining in varieties of colors from blues and grays, pinks and yellows, to black. Marble of extreme purity will be a bright white.

Coming through all the hard-pressed days, all the scars and tears cried that we carry to reach his presence are vanquished because our new name is perfected into a pure white stone interlocked into a oneness that no enemy or disaster can break apart. Bodies will be raised with no sign of abuse or wounds. No one is blind, deaf, or crippled. Those weakened in life are strong. All are clean and whole by what the Lord has led them through, testified in each name presented in their white stone.

The white stone is not given without the manna. The disciples asked Jesus what they should do so that they may work the works of God. Jesus said to believe in him whom God has sent. What is the sign so we can see and believe? The fathers ate manna in the wilderness. Jesus then told them it was not Moses who has given the manna but the Father, who gives you the true bread out of heaven. "For the bread of God is that which comes down out of heaven, and gives life to the world." They responded, "Lord, always give us this bread." Jesus said to them, "I am the bread of life; he who comes to Me will not hunger, and he who believes in Me will never thirst" (John 6:28–35). The hidden manna is in his presence with us.

The church became a shelter but with a higher purpose. Endowed with being able to say, "God sees you. The Lord knows you," hope is brought into the depths of those who never had anyone to pray for them. Yet as the world becomes more connected than ever, we are lonelier than ever. Media images are absent the friend seeking the best for the eternal soul, the presence of a father guarding, the quiet spirit of a mother's presence, the grandparents sensitive to their every choice, the neighbor knowing them by name. Dislodged from the context, a heart in its isolation has no understanding of what God is bringing together.

According to a 2018 Cigna study,[2] more than half of America feels lonely, and younger Americans born between the mid-1990s and early 2000s are the loneliest. Health insurer Cigna's nationwide survey found that 54 percent of respondents said they feel like no one actually knows them well; 56 percent said the people who surround them "are not necessarily with them"; and about 40 percent said they "lack companionship," their "relationships are not meaningful," and they feel "isolated from others." We know each other less than ever, presenting in symptoms of health and depressive issues as the enemy tries to silence the light that interlocks lives.

Loneliness was the first issue that newly created man faced in the garden. God says it is not good to be so alone. Manna brings his body to interact together, sharing the troubles and celebrations of the soul. It keeps us less lonely as part of something much greater than ourselves. He not only gets people out of their isolation, he brings together people of all kinds. We meet toddlers, ninety-year-olds, teenagers, and middle-aged mothers. We talk with older married couples, taking in their perspective, as well as with youth considering their futures.

2. Jenkins, "Americans Lonely."

Your position has changed. In him all things hold together. "Having been knit together in love ... resulting in a true knowledge of God's mystery, that is, Christ Himself" (Col 2:2). Anguish does not come in believing the Lord of all creation. It comes from those around us not wanting the faith to be established, not wanting us to be established, encouraged, or discerning. The enemy comes mocking at opportune times saying, "Where is your leader now? You are all alone." Society gives up on waiting for God as if there is another hope. Or they take on the work of their own salvation, thinking self-help is a match for spiritual warfare, which is already lost if it succeeds in taking eyes off seeking the Lord. He took a diverse group of men and equipped them to become a sanctified unity by bringing each to value their part in God's purpose more than their own differences. The promise never changes; in light, under sediments, carried away, broken in pieces, the word remains unswerving, dependable, preserving us in the world as we move through the fire, the flood, the quaking land.

We are called to take part with Jesus reattaching a fallen world to God. Yet at the end of just one day we are aware of our many shortcomings, much less can we reach the end of our lives without his righteousness to stand before God. To those who gathered wanting to silence him and put him to death, Jesus responded, "Truly, truly, I say to you, he who hears My word, and believes Him who sent Me, has eternal life, and does not come into judgment, but has passed out of death into life" (John 5:24). He at once declares his protection of those who give their trust to him as he extends the invitation, because life is what he wants for his doubters too. The greatness of an infinite Lord is that he will never lose his unlimited nature to uphold unchanging standards. God can never be bound by finite premises.

When Samuel said to Saul, "you have rejected the word of the Lord and the Lord has rejected you from being king" (1 Sam 15:26), it was because Saul continued in his own ideas, thinking he was pleasing the Lord yet ignoring what the Lord wanted of him. The word of God had gone from him. The crown on his head was meaningless. The heart becomes lukewarm if the heart settles on the surface for too long. Looking only at appearance, claiming to believe, like Saul we can think we are fine. Jesus says they are poor, blind, naked, and unaware that they are lukewarm (Rev 3:15). The heart that is cold toward the Lord has no interest in the things of God. Wickedness abounds upheld by their unbelief. But they yet may see the emptiness of it and become heated for Jesus more easily than the lukewarm, who consider their own ways as God's ways.

A temple official in Jerusalem had Jeremiah beaten and put in the stocks at the Upper Gate of Benjamin for a day. After this, Jeremiah expresses lament over the difficulties that speaking God's word has caused him. He was the target of mockery. Then he speaks of how the word becomes a fire burning in his heart and he is unable to hold it in if he tries to shut down the word of the Lord and not mention God's name. He cannot hold back (Jer 20:9). The hope within glows brightest in times of adversity, bringing about the deepest pleas. Longing to be released from what plagues us, hearts burn when Jesus is near. He took a loaf of bread and suddenly the eyes of those he walked beside recognized Jesus. They said to one another, "Were not our hearts burning within us while He was speaking to us on the road, while He was explaining the scriptures to us?" (Luke 24:32). They went back to Jerusalem to seek fellowship with the disciples and asked Jesus to come spend time with them.

The very ones who think they are religious will disregard what we feel; they do not see us, do not hear. They will make us outcasts. Hope keeps taking the next breath, choosing to follow Jesus. The burning in our hearts when we hear his voice raises us, weathers us, transports us, and changes us because we are not content to be lukewarm. It may begin as a solitary step taken in a lonely world, yet gradually we see the others increasing around us staking out God's territory.

These things I have spoken to you so that you may be kept from stumbling (John 16:1). Jesus didn't want the troubles to interrupt your walk, make you scared, or feel small. The mind hardens in those who won't let his words be written on their hearts through the heat and pressure of metamorphism. They ignore the hurting and the yearning deep within needing his mercy. There are impenetrable layers all around their heart as they cry for the rocks to hide them and wish for death rather than confront their own faults. When they are scorched with great heat they assert themselves against all that God has spoken.

Not persuaded by the Lord, hardened hearts resist being fit into their place building the kingdom. Scripture informs that out of our hearts comes grief (John 14:1), desires (Matt 5:28), joy (Eph 5:19), understanding (Isa 6:10), and faith (Rom 10:10). Hearts can suffer in all these ways. But forged by the stone crafter, faith listens for him, strengthening the ability to rejoice, knowing that trials produce perseverance, character, and hope. And hope does not disappoint us because our story does not end there (Rom 5:3–5). By nature we are inclined to be our own savior, work out our own solutions, and do our own will. The difficulty in trusting the Lord who goes ahead of us to make a way is seen in the Israelites under pressure. Until hearts are awakened, "They will say, 'It's hopeless! For we are going to follow our own plans, and each of us will act according to the stubbornness of his evil heart'" (Jer 18:12). "But because of your stubbornness and unrepentant heart you are storing up wrath for yourself in the day of wrath and revelation of the righteous judgment of God" (Rom 2:5).

How can a young man keep his ways pure? By keeping it according to the Lord's word (Ps 119:9–11). "He did evil because he had not set his heart on seeking the Lord" (2 Chro 12:14). Being renewed in our minds is an all-encompassing exhortation. It requires bodies and minds dedicated to not being conformed to the spiritual age of the world. But be transformed by testing to discern what is the will of God (Rom 12:1–2). Knowing the Lord's will enabled David to sit down and write, "your servant has found courage to pray this prayer to you." Do as you promised, he says to God, so that your name will be great forever (2 Sam 7:25–27). Call on the Lord to do what he has already pledged to do for us. "Remember Jesus Christ, risen from the dead" (2 Tim 2:8).

"Remember His wonderful deeds which He has done, His marvels and the judgments from His mouth (1 Chr 16:12).

When we win a race, it is not about the hardships that got us there. It's about the result. The white stone inscribed with a name known only to the recipient serves as a pass to a prestigious banquet only attended after completion of the race. Winning begins with hearing him as he knows us. Jesus speaks to "he who has an ear, let him hear what the Spirit says to the churches" (Rev 2:7).

The Shema is a call to listen. "Hear, O Israel! The Lord is our God, the Lord is one!" (Deut 6:4). Because God cannot be seen but can be heard, *shema* means to hear, pay attention, understand, and respond by gathering to him. Moses insistently told the people to hear the Lord. "Then the Lord spoke to you from the midst of the fire; you heard the sound of words, but you saw no form—only a voice" (Deut 4:12). "See, I am setting before you today a blessing and a curse: the blessing, if you listen to the commandments of the Lord your God, which I am commanding you today; and the curse, if you do not listen to the commandments of the Lord your God" (Deut 11:26-28). His words deliver us and protect us from the enemies (2 Sam 22:2-3).

God connects with us through conversation. Speaking tells about who we are, but we learn who he is when we open ourselves in wonderment and listen. "If you listen . . ." was Moses' insistent reminder. "Everyone must be quick to hear, slow to speak and slow to anger" (Jas 1:19). Hearing heals divisions. Hearing is a redemptive act. To be heard is to feel that we are known and we matter. "Blessed is the man who listens to me, watching daily at my gates, waiting at my doorposts" (Prov 8:34).

The times we feel distant from God we have been given words to speak to ourselves and the words will renew our minds. "Why are you in despair, O my soul? Hope in God, for I shall yet praise Him" (Ps 42:11). "Bless the Lord, O my soul, and forget none of His benefits" (Ps 103:2). "I will watch expectantly for the Lord; I will wait for the God of my salvation. My God will hear me" (Mic 7:7). "I will confess my transgressions to the Lord" (Ps 32:5). "This I recall to my mind, therefore I have hope" (Lam 3:21).

The Rock from Which You Were Hewn

Set your minds on things above (Col 3:2). Directing the mind to these thoughts is a command from God to rouse your heart, relate to the world through heaven's story, seek what is good, appreciate a friend, a sunny day, and rains that refresh. Notice the power of the Creator to change rocks into shining gems.

11

Buried

So he cut out two stone tablets like the former ones. (Exod 34:4)

METAMORPHIC ROCKS FORM IN the heart of Earth's action, in mountain ranges during the collisions of continental plates, along zones where the slabs grind unseen deep below the surface, next to magma chambers radiating heat, and along mid-ocean ridges, where hot corrosive seawater rushes through the ocean's crust. Metamorphic rocks witness what can only be imagined. We don't see the extreme pressure and temperature beneath the surface, but we witness the result.

The rocks were once igneous, sedimentary, or another metamorphic rock, now changed because of pressures in the elements around them forming new minerals and different appearances. Many combinations of temperature and pressures cement the mud and clay settling into sedimentary rock called shale, for example, added to clay art projects. Shale buried under more pressure changes into the metamorphic rock slate, useful for roofs and flooring. Less heat and pressure and it may become schist, used as a touchstone to test the purity of gold alloys.

Earth cycles rocks through continual erosion, sedimentation, burial, metamorphism, mountain building, and collisions to align young rocks with older rocks. As each generation passes through the Lord's ordained process of unearthing a soul to refine it, the Great Commission is written on the corridors by all who went before us. When the Israelites entered the land of Canaan, a new generation shouted the blessings that had come to them through Moses. The Lord first redeemed them, then showed them how they were to live. Every generation that followed carried the blessings in their soul.

When King David spoke to his people about his son, Solomon, being chosen to build the temple, he said, "The task is great, because this palatial structure is not for man but for the Lord God." All Solomon's resources were provided by the Earth for the temple of his God. Gold, silver, bronze, iron, wood, gems of many colors, and large quantities of fine stone and marble (1 Chr 29:1–2). Hewn stone was used. Blocks were prepared at the quarry and no hammer, chisel, or any iron tool was heard at the temple site while it was being built (1 Kgs 6:7). The difficult experiences that have refined us will no longer echo in our minds. The sounds of weeping will no longer be heard (Rev 21:4). They will be forgotten.

Hewn stone is stone changed for a specific purpose. But altars of stone should never be built of hewn stones because wielding our tools on it profanes it (Exod 20:25; Deut 27:5). An altar is a place to present offerings, which are acceptable only because of what the Lord has done. The stones of the altar represent the work of God and his kingdom, unhewn by human hands. If mallets and chisels were to fit stone, it could open the way to making counterfeit glory, such as the bricks used to build the tower of Babel. They said, "Come, let us build for ourselves a city, and a tower whose top will reach into heaven, and let us make for ourselves a name" (Gen 11:4). It was a false opinion that came to mankind's thoughts to reach God's heaven by his own works, rolling out humanistic thinking as a solution—education, jobs, government aide, law enforcement—baffled that the world's pain is not fixed by more funding, more rationalizing reasons to validate every behavior.

Only the work of the Father in sacrificing his Son on the altar of mercy opens the gate (Eph 2:8). "And do not suppose that you can say to yourselves, 'We have Abraham for our father,' for I say to you that from these stones God is able to raise up children to Abraham" (Matt 3:9). From the very foundation of the rocks that support all creation, acceptable worship of God is done in God's ways. The stone of an altar is the way God created it to be. It requires no work of mankind to be made acceptable.

It was Israel's first tragedy when the tablets God wrote upon were broken at Mount Sinai because the people were dancing around a golden calf. Moses came down the mountain holding the stone tablets in his two hands. When he saw what the people were doing, he threw them to shatter on the ground. It is said that the broken tablets were placed in the holy ark along with the second tablets Moses brought to the people (Talmud Bava Batra 14b). Although broken, they too were esteemed and kept in the most sacred place. The nation protected both the broken and the whole tablets as they journeyed through the wilderness.

As a symbol of the chambers of a human heart, the broken pieces of a life coexist with the whole pieces sought from the Lord to make us complete. Even within the holiest of places, brokenness is carried within us. The mistakes of the past remain as regrets. The aching loss of a loved one becomes a part of us. We move through life with both the broken parts of our world and the grace of our God that gives mercy beyond what is humanly possible.

After breaking the first tablets, Moses walked back up the mountain, perhaps remembering being on the mountain when first the Lord came to him in a fire blazing from a bush and said, "I have indeed seen the misery of my people in Egypt. I have heard them crying" (Exod 3:2-7). Moses climbs again to intercede with God on behalf of his people, showing the need to be given a chance to return to the Lord, whose compassion abounds in understanding. It is no longer about the enemy of the people of Israel. It has become about God opening the heavens for them to know him and send them to bring light to the nations. From that mountain the world was given the concept of God being one living being who created us all, who wants to bless us, give us Sabbath rest from our labors, and reaches to include everyone. Humanity's hope was answered with redemption in the world to come.

The heart moves to and from the broken ways to the perfect will of God, telling us where we come from and to whom we will give a final accounting. "So teach us to number our days," Moses prayed, "that we may present to you a heart of wisdom" (Ps 90:12). People who see their days are limited look back at the times that were regretfully wasted. They wish there had been more moments with family and friends to express gratitude and kindness. They long to undo decisions and instead choose God's way. Awareness of mortality liberates from the pettiness that causes rifts in relationships and chases things that disappear tomorrow. It changes how we apportion the time we give of ourselves as we finish the race speaking with clarity about what is most precious in the heart.

It is a consciousness that comes to elderly hearts that have much to remind us about Moses' prayer. "Let your clothes be white all the time, and let not oil be lacking on your head" (Eccl 9:8). The white robe feasts mean we have come to the Lord to cleanse us through his atonement. The oil is not lacking because the Lord generously pours out his Holy Spirit when we draw near to him. When our works are approved by heaven, we eat our bread in gladness and drink our wine with a cheerful heart (Eccl 9:7).

To be truly holy in the Lord means to be fully identified with the chambers of our inner heart. We are not to disconnect from the world or deny the broken shards. We may mourn what we won't see fulfilled. It may be grandchildren growing up, a career unfulfilled, or a move to a wished-for place denied. The tablets that became broken and the whole tablets serve to teach us that both are important to the Lord. The ark was placed in the holy of holies, in the presence of an angel, in the stillness of the aftermath of the tearing pain hell has caused. It was set in the sight of our own smallness, where awe for his word, the gift that came down from heaven, is to be placed in our hands.

On the path of knowing God there are uneven jagged rocks with sharp edges demanding us to be accepting of the unacceptable. Being restored to become images of God, our souls instinctively cheer with a sense of victory when a child is lifted out of a well, a bird is freed from a net, a runner crosses the finish line. Freedom celebrates the ability to fulfill what they are meant to do in lives given by God. But we cannot always save someone's dying child and sometimes we earn only last place. The most awkward of tasks is finding words that offer comfort. We seek frantically for a right response. We have to do something. At these times, a traditional prayer in Israel is reached for to say, "May the Omnipresent comfort you among the mourners of Zion and Jerusalem." Only God, who knows the hidden innermost heart, is truly capable of fathoming such grief and provide refuge to our mortality. We call upon God to console the afflicted because we cannot.

HaMakom, the Omnipresent, literally means "The Place." When death and despair come, we pray that the bereaved revive with awareness that God is everywhere, even in places stricken with grief. Our broken places are still the place of God. Because of God's oneness, even passing into death is part of his plan. No one's purpose is lost. The soul is eternal, returning to its Creator in the place of heaven, which would comfort us if we could glimpse its beauty.

Each loss wraps someone in mourning, an all-encompassing sadness wandering through a house that is irrevocably empty no matter how many people fill it. We can tell ourselves all the right words to maintain faith in God's goodness and remind ourselves that in the next world everything will be resolved, but our heart will still feel so grieved that we remain restricted by pain because there is no other place we are able be. The spirit tries to send its transcendent faith through our being, but the mind says it is senseless. What happened is wrong. Pain overtakes like an ocean, in small ripples of sadness and in leagues of waves crashing in wrenching sobs. Pushed beneath the surface to be trapped with pain we did not have before brings us into a new struggle of making God's will our own will. Mourning tripping back and forth between the loneliness of depression and propelling to seek the Lord's comfort is a natural progression of resolving the conflict, helped by being able to honestly say, "I hurt. Let me cry."

The Lord understands we need a time to mourn, but a limited time. Even so, young Joseph's father refused to be comforted when he was told Joseph was probably dead (Gen 37:35). The refusal to be comforted sounded again when Jeremiah prophesied 1,100 years after Rachel died. "A voice is heard in Ramah, mourning and great weeping, Rachel weeping for her children and refusing to be comforted because her children are no more." Accepting the comfort would mean accepting the loss. Knowing the Lord is omnipresent, they refused to give up hoping and they were justified. Jacob said he would mourn the rest of his days, longing for his son, unaccepting of his loss. Joseph was alive and restored to his father. "There is hope for your future," declares the Lord, telling Rachel there is no need to weep. "Your children will return to their own land" (Jer 31:15–17).

Jeremiah's prophecy received a second accomplishment when Herod slaughtered the male children in Bethlehem trying to prevent Jesus from becoming a king (Matt 2:18). Rachel had died in Bethlehem, birthing Benjamin, the completion of the twelve tribes (Gen 35:19). Bethlehem is on the West Bank, about six miles south of Jerusalem. David was born here. It's where the prophet Samuel crowned David as king. Jesus was born in Bethlehem. Mary and Joseph returned to Bethlehem, coming from Nazareth in northern Israel to register in a national tax census (Luke 2:1–7). They had to travel ninety miles to the city of Joseph's ancestors, south along the flatlands of the Jordan River, westward over the hills surrounding Jerusalem, and on into Bethlehem past the tomb Jacob set for Rachel's burial. Traveling several days, they went up from Nazareth to Bethlehem, climbing upward through the Judean Hills.

The rocks of the Judean Hills reach downward to the western banks of the Dead Sea, the lowest point in the world, sitting at 420 feet below sea level, and to the Jordan Valley Rift, which marks the modern border between Palestine and Jordan. The valley was formed when the Arabian tectonic plate moved away from Africa and separated the plates. The hills include the Mount of Olives and the place the story of David and Goliath occurred. Bethlehem sits on a ridge of the Judean Hills. The name means "House of Bread," where Jesus came from saying, "I am the bread of life." Jesus made it possible for the dead to live, for Rachel to rejoice again and Jacob be comforted where he once grieved the death of his beloved wife (Gen 48:7). Believers are people who do not grieve as those without hope (1 Thess 4:13) even when all the evidence may tell us there is no chance of our world being whole again and we must accept a fate of irretrievable loss.

Even as the world recedes as we age, the bread, the manna he gifts to us, remains fresh and present. Hope of any more goals in this life fades with the years. The grasses grow over the spaces we once stood. There are senior citizen centers that offer activities, recreation, and games, but we have lived life with meaningful vision and goals. We worked toward dreams and significant purpose. Recreation and memories are no substitute for that sense of meaning that defines our place in life.

When Moses approached the end of his life, he told the people he could no longer continue with them. He faced his own death as he looked across at the promised land from the peak of Mount Nebo. "You shall not go over there," the Lord told him. The Lord did not give him permission to continue across the Jordan with his people (Deut 34:1–4). Instead of feeling that the best of his days had been taken away, Moses identified his next achievement was no longer about providing and liberating, but about giving spiritual mentorship. In the opening chapter of Deuteronomy he becomes a teacher expounding on all that the Lord had done for them. He's now a man teaching about the law's power in the past and speaking of the future to the next generation, anticipating their challenges as they continued ascending to the promise of God. In his last days, at 120 years of age, his words were still full of the passion God graced him with when he first began the journey. "Remember," he says again and again. "Listen to the voice of God. Rejoice in what he has given you." The legacy became a continual resource for his people, shaping lives made better into the future.

Among the aged there are those who took to heart God's guidance to "Remember also your Creator in the days of your youth, before the evil days come and the years draw near when you will say, 'I have no delight in them'" (Eccl 12:1). Their years centered on the Lord as the heart of their world. They may have studied the vast treasury of Scripture or gathered in groups to contemplate abundant sources of learning. For these elders, working earned a living but the goal of life was always about relationship. No longer preoccupied with the cares of the hurried world, the shadow of death becomes a valley of light. Anticipation of the world of heaven comes nearer.

Elders are in the most spiritual place in the life cycle. They inhabit stillness. In living rooms, nursing homes, or kitchens they welcome visitors to sit and talk, remembering all that God has done; how he's answered prayer, delivered from crisis, and the meaning that can be found when he has not answered a prayer. Elders become a place of communion where we come to learn perspective on the migrations of stones revealing appointed times to return again to the Lord in repentance. They can be a place of hearing how to pray for those who harmed us, as Jesus prayed breathing his last on the cross. Those who know God look at the dust of the ground and see living stones building a temple of glory, weathered and refined with experiences only the Lord perceives, inscribed in names embedded in a perfected stone. We come to want the dignity elders of the Lord carry as men and women, the kind of relationships they've fostered, and the peaceful assurance that settles even when their bodies are signaling the end of their work on Earth.

A fulfilled life depends entirely on obedience to the Lord. The momentum of youth and health cannot be compared to measure the value of the days ahead. Strength and health have changed through the weathering and erosion of years. Jesus is still Lord, still sovereign, with us, asking our trust to follow him into the realm of the holy songs of angels. Rather than deal with suffering, society unravels the virtue of God and promotes individual rights to choose suicide, calling it a dignified euthanasia. It is opting out of relationship with God before we have a chance to fathom God's words to us. Ending a life when pain is beyond endurance is not compassion. True compassion walks beside a person and shares the burden of finding strength. God's long-suffering servants endured torture, imprisonment, being in chains, dropped to the bottom of a well, and witnessed horrible deaths of loved ones. Should Paul in his days, despairing even for his life, or John, alone on a cold lonely island with no hope of ever going home to friends and family, have opted to die instead of blessing all the world because they trusted to reach for God's sufficient grace?

Who can say what suffering will be assigned to each life asked to follow Jesus to the very end. He told us we would have a cross to carry as we pass through each stage of life. The furnace of affliction may be an illness, bereavement, a family member going astray, unexpected financial loss, or the bludgeoning of persecution. The furnace sanctifies what is brought through it and answers the wish for joy to be known again. All will pass except these three: faith, hope, and love. The greatest of these is love (1 Cor 13:13). This is how Jesus endured his suffering—for the joy before him. That joy is the salvation of us.

Society's ever-expanding idea of personal autonomy fails to remember the constricted moment of Israel's decision to step into the sea, pressed by a pursuing army, choosing to be God's bondservants, to be found in him, fully wanting his power to part the sea. While we have choice, we have responsibility to affirm life in God. Legalized euthanasia sends permission to teenagers considering suicide in their cry for mercy. A person living on their own terms may commit suicide to escape the unbearable, but the soul cannot return to the body. There will not be another time given for them to place belief in God's desire for their victory.

It never means there are not understandable moments when someone believes death would be better than enduring what has been put upon them. King Saul fell on his sword rather than be captured and tortured by the Philistines. Samson willingly died in his final act of killing off enemies of his people. We count on God to understand the wish for virtue chosen over an enemy's desecrations. We pray for the lives that are not honored, souls that feel unknown and have no one standing under the burden with them. Love was not made visible in their lives and they have no capacity to believe there is anything better than escaping the pain. Even those with faith do not have strength to resist pain that there has been no way to imagine.

We show empathy for those who left us too soon. We pray God never forgets the many good intentions their lives held. But we grieve the way they lost the greatest offer of God to bring beauty out of the ashes. We're denied our opportunity to be needed in the process of life and death and the privilege of helping to propel a soul to higher heaven. We are left filled with pity and the lost chance at intervention, not with a satisfaction that they have done the right thing.

Who is there to show us how to have no fear when it is our turn to enter eternity, knowing there is no final end when we leave behind our bodies to return to dust? When Jacob reached his time to die, he was there to bless his sons because of all that God had said to him in his life. Then he instructed them saying, "I am about to be gathered to my people." He asked to be entombed with his fathers in the cave in Canaan where Abraham, Sarah, Isaac, Rebekah, and Leah were buried (Gen 49). His bond with his family did not end for him because he was dying. He blessed his offspring with every expectation of God to complete his plan and reunite them and their descendants. There is no separation from God's love for those who rest their trust in the Lord. All those who have passed and knew where they were going now emanate from their seats in the world to come. The rough places have been smoothed into brilliant white stone.

12

Emptied

So with the stones he built an altar in the name of the Lord.
(1 Kgs 18:32)

IN THE DEPTHS OF the Earth rocks are melting. As more magma seeps into a volcano's chamber, the pressure becomes explosive and the melted rocks burst out in the eruption. Cooling, they crystallize into igneous rocks. Weather and erosion begin and the cycle starts again.

As long as there is more magma pooling into a volcano's chamber, there is the possibility of another eruption to relieve the pressure. Gases, ash, and light-colored rock burst in a fury first, from the least-dense, top layer of the magma chamber. Dark dense rock from the lower chambers ruptures in high columns and ash and pumice fall, blanketing the Earth thousands of miles around. Fast-moving currents of hot magma hit the ground and hurl downhill, moving at speeds reaching up to 430 miles an hour. Knocking down and incinerating anything in its path, it leaves the sun in the sky shining weakly through plumes of haze that can stay in the air for weeks. The eruptions will continue until the magma is emptied and the chamber collapses as a crater.

Sin will perpetuate in the human soul until the Lord returns and it is entirely emptied, cast into fire to be forever consumed. "For a fire is kindled in my anger, and burns to the lowest part of Sheol, and consumes the earth with its yield, and sets on fire the foundations of the mountains" (Deut 32:22). The Lord comes to the gate and the channels of the sea appear. The foundations of the world are laid bare at the blast of his breath (2 Sam 22:16).

God prepared us for this and gave to us the Spirit as a pledge (2 Cor 5:5). The disciples came through every fear, hard pressed, perplexed, struck down, filtering through moments of doubt (John 20:19; 2 Cor 4:8–9; Matt 28:17). Yet Paul says we can always be of good courage. Confident even in death, to be away from the body is to be in the presence of the Lord, the Earth embraces our bodies returning to dust and our spirit returning to God who gave it (Eccl 12:7). The path opens as it did when the Red Sea parted. Angels escort each soul, a convoy of protection through the atmosphere where Satan rules, so that we are not alone as they carry us safely to the third heaven (Luke 16:22).

Those who die in the Lord continue waiting expectantly for him to return to Earth and fulfill the destiny of his holiness. They cry out from under the altar wondering, "How long, O Lord, holy and true, will You refrain from judging and avenging our blood on those who dwell on the earth?" (Rev 6:9–10). They are in hope with believers on Earth looking forward to the world to come, waiting for the trumpet sound and the perishable to put on the imperishable. They hear angels rejoice whenever someone is newly born into the Lord. The wrenching sobs on Earth in a heart calling on the Lord sound as joy in heaven.

In a vision John saw an eagle and heard it announcing the woes to come as it flew through the midst of the heavens. Family die, friends suffer, phone lines go dead, communication breaks down, the future is undependable. The news reports that someone has announced a solution, coming as a deceiver pointing to himself as the solution. The Antichrist speaks of his own powers and targets followers who are weakened and desperate for hope. They did not believe the people the Lord had sent to them. God gave them over to the deluding influence and they believe what is false. They will see judgment (2 Thess 2:10–12).

There is no more delay. Their minds inflame with resistance because their hearts had not been circumcised through wanting truth. "O Lord, do not your eyes look for truth? You have smitten them, but they did not weaken; you have consumed them, but they refused to take correction. They have made their faces harder than rock; they have refused to repent" (Jer 5:3). The last battle on Earth will reveal the living God, previewed by Elijah, who said to Israel, "If the Lord is God then follow him." God showed himself by sending fire from heaven that consumed the burnt offerings, wood, stones, dust, and water on the altar (1 Kgs 18).

When the seventh angel sounds his trumpet, the kingdoms of man become kingdoms belonging to Jesus forever (Rev 11:15), as happened in Jericho when the priests blew trumpets and circled the city seven times. At the last blast, the city fell with the sound of rocks falling and people wailing. The hearts of the people in the city had melted because of hearing all that God in heaven above and on Earth below had done for Israel (Josh 2:24). "And even the one who is valiant, whose heart is like the heart of a lion, will completely lose heart" (2 Sam 17:10). God instructed Israel's military to allow those who are faint-hearted to return to their homes and enter into private prayer with the Lord so that they don't influence the other soldiers to faint (Deut 20:8). The hearts of those who stand have been refined in the very fiber of their being through a life of fires, consuming doubts, and agendas. They follow the extreme influence of generations who charted the narrow path for those who follow.

"The heavens will disappear with a roar; the elements will be destroyed by fire, and the earth and everything done in it will be laid bare" (2 Pet 3:10). "He is the One who touches the land so that it melts" (Amos 9:5). "The earth is broken asunder. The earth is split through. The earth is shaken violently" (Isa 24:19). "He only is my rock and my salvation, my stronghold; I shall not be greatly shaken . . . Trust in Him at all times, O people; pour out your heart before Him; God is a refuge for us" (Ps 62:2, 8). "My words will not pass away," Jesus said (Luke 21:33).

Moses' last song to Israel asks them to join in praising the wonderful name of the Lord our God (Deut 32:3). When he finished, he said to the people to always remember this song. "Let it be a warning that you must teach your children to obey God's word because his law can give you a long life in the land you are going into." Peter carried the reminder. "Beloved, do not be surprised at the fiery ordeal among you, which comes upon you for your testing, as though some strange thing were happening to you; but to the degree that you share the sufferings of Christ, keep on rejoicing, so that also at the revelation of His glory you may rejoice with exultation" (1 Pet 4:12). "And if it is with difficulty that the righteous is saved, what will become of the godless man and the sinner?" Entrust your soul to a faithful Creator (vv. 18–19). God sees you. He longs to hear your voice.

Singing the song that has been brought into harmony from all the discordant notes of life will ring out exultant as he opens heaven and the elements tremble. Rocks underground catch on each other, pushing against each other with such force they break apart, causing seismic waves to shake the planet. Buildings whose foundations are on liquefying sand will suddenly lose support. Cracking foundations, damaging structures, land is pushed upward by pressure, pushing soil through Earth's crust to enter buildings, dismantling electrical services. Buildings fold under the force. Bridges tilt on the sloping ground. River and lake water slides across the land, spreading large cracks in the ground to topple roads and services such as water, natural gas, sewerage, and telecommunications. Buried tanks and manholes will float. Flood levees and dams will collapse.

"For it will come upon all those who dwell on the face of all the earth. But keep on the alert at all times, praying that you may have strength to escape all these things that are about to take place, and to stand before the Son of Man" (Luke 21:35–36). The Earth dissolves. The sky falls. The singers continue their praise as the dust settles and there is his new creation and his living stones, each with a new name glowing in his glory.

Jesus forewarned of the terrible time of shaking, kingdom against kingdom in the fire of his wrath. The prophets warned that the Earth shall quake, the sun and moon darken, and stars withdraw their shining when the power of heaven opens. Darkness came with the giving of the law at Mount Sinai. The mountain shook under God's presence, shrouded by thick billowing smoke flashing with thunder (Exod 19:16–18). Lightning bolts vibrated between clouds, striking from the ground, heating the air as hot as 50,000 degrees Fahrenheit and echoing waves of thunder along paths traveling miles away, moving in light faster than sound. Clouds collide. Updrafts and downdrafting winds fly in all directions.

When Jesus died, the Earth again violently shook, rocks were split, and the veil of the temple was torn open from top to bottom (Matt 27:51). The job of the high priest ended with that sound as Jesus became our highest priest. At his death Earth darkened at midday. The prophet Zephaniah saw judgment as a day of darkness, gloom, clouds, and thick darkness (Zeph 1:15). Isaiah beheld the day of the Lord coming to lay the land desolate and exterminate sinners (Isa 13:9). A depression settles onto Earth. The sky opens. Armies of angels appear. The mystery of God is accomplished. The people everywhere know Jesus is Lord, some bowing in fear and condemnation, some bowing in worship and gladness.

John looked and saw "a great multitude which no one could count . . . standing before the throne and before the Lamb, clothed in white robes" (Rev 7:9). Their prayers for cleansing had been answered. "Purify me with hyssop and I shall be clean. Wash me and I shall be whiter than snow" (Ps 5:7). "Blessed are the dead who die in the Lord from now on" (Rev 14:13). They are kept within holy light. They serve in the court of the Lord, never tired, never feeling the heat of the sun. Filling us with all the light, the kindness, the restful wholeness of health that he wanted us to have, Jesus wipes away the tears. We wept for our failures and wasted moments. We wept for the sorrow others endure. We wept in relief of such great a salvation. God reconciles the times of weeping, then takes away the sadness for those he tells to depart from him and they are lost forever. Finally all tears of those he gathered near are dried.

"For this reason I endure all things for the sake of those who are chosen, so that they also may obtain the salvation which is in Christ Jesus and with it eternal glory" (2 Tim 2:10). Paul understood that the Lord alone has a kingdom without end. Adam had been warned away from death when the Lord told him not to eat from the tree of knowledge because "on the day that you eat from it, you will surely die" (Gen 2:17). The verse does not mean that the fruit would immediately kill them. Adam and Eve went on to live for a long time after eating the forbidden fruit. The verse seems to mean "on the day that you eat from the fruit you will become mortal" and become beings that die. Once they ate from the tree, they were banished from Eden "lest they eat from the tree of life and live forever." Humanity in the garden was poised in an undetermined state between mortality and immortality with two mysterious trees defining our grand saga. God desired that they eventually eat from the tree of life and his Son Jesus made the choice between life and death again possible. The new vision is our healing.

All stones begin as common rocks. Some find fame, like America's Plymouth Rock, an igneous granite marking the start of the Plymouth colony in 1620. Or the Blarney Stone set in the battlement of Blarney Castle in Cork, Ireland. Legend has it this local block of limestone is part of the Stone of Destiny, the rock upon which the kings of Scotland were crowned. The sailing stones in a remote dried lake bed in California called Racetrack Playa each bear a woman's name. The large sedimentary dolomite rocks came to fame by moving along the desert ground with no gravitational cause, leaving long trails in the dried mud. The forty thousand interlocking basalt columns of the Giant's Causeway provide stepping stones into the sea on the north coast of Ireland, formed from volcanic fissures centuries ago. The monolithic Rock of Gibraltar is limestone cresting more than a thousand feet high with a labyrinth of tunnels and caves at the southern tip of the Iberian Peninsula in the Mediterranean Sea, giving rest to more than a quarter million migratory birds crossing the sea and desert, flowers of chickweed and thyme, breeding places for partridges and kestrels. Families of Barbary macaques thrive on the high cliffs layered over sedimentary strata.

The ancient stone that took generations of weathering, erosion, and pressures to form to be used to block the tomb of Jesus became known as the stone an angel touched, an angel who had worshipped Jesus since the beginning, watched as his creation beat him and spit on him, but held back his power to chasten the oppressors so that Jesus could save. A sudden earthquake struck Earth when the angel descended from heaven to roll away the stone and victory emerged (Matt 28:1). Rocks that the Lord chooses to purify for building his kingdom are formed in the heart of life's action, during the collisions of unseen forces, along zones where ideals grind unseen deep below the surface, and next to beliefs radiating heat.

Highly esteeming our prayers for strength, Jesus gives a white stone engraved with a name that is testimony of being sustained by manna from heaven because we could not do it by ourselves. What was needed to get us to the finish line moved so deeply within us; only the Lord knows the truth of our experiences. The new name reflects the battles we have come through, the conquering of other desires, the loss we have suffered, the ways he has disciplined, and the forgiveness we sought. The name will identify who we have transformed into because of being led by providence (2 Pet 1:4). The name is what God sees in us beyond our tattered rags, his redeemed creation, restored by his Son. "My Grief" becomes "His Mercy," a shared knowing between you and the Lord, who was with you every step.

Only the Lord can fashion that stone. In the book of Daniel, God gave Nebuchadnezzar, king of Babylon, a dream that used the imagery of a "stone cut without hands" (Dan 2). The king saw a gigantic statue made of four materials, from its gold head and silver chest and arms to its feet of mingled iron and clay. As he watched, a stone not cut by human hands destroyed the statue and became a mountain filling the whole world. Daniel interpreted the dream to the king, revealing the statue represented four successive kingdoms beginning with Babylon and the stone and mountain signified a kingdom established by God.

"In the days of those kings the God of heaven will set up a kingdom which will never be destroyed, and that kingdom will not be left for another people; it will crush and put an end to all these kingdoms, but it will itself endure forever" (Dan 2:44–45). Paul quoted Isaiah 45:23, foretelling "at the name of Jesus every knee will bow, of those who are in heaven and on earth and under the earth, and that every tongue will confess that Jesus Christ is Lord, to the glory of God the Father" (Phil 2:10–11). "I have kept the faith," Paul said (2 Tim 4:7). In continuous struggle every day, he held on to eternal life, the gift held out to you to receive and hold.

Jesus is glorified by the vast number of the redeemed, from every place on Earth, from every generation, so many no one can count. He sees the fruits of his suffering, the lament turned into song because he wept with us. Jesus has brought every one of his safely home. Everybody's story will be there. The entire genealogy of Jesus, more than forty lives listed in Matthew 1:1–6 representing broken lives fraught with trials, are all there. Every one of them was tested, cleansed, set free by the truth, and refined to fulfill the glorious joy. David, who was an adulterer, Moses, who was a murderer, Hagar, who was abandoned, the Samaritan woman whose life was discordant, Tamar, whose clothing was violently torn, the thief whom Jesus invited, all now robed in white, in joy because God sees their hearts. The widows, the lepers, the blind and crippled, every loss, every disappointment, fear, loneliness, and betrayal, is made whole as they praise God and the Lamb for their salvation.

He has wiped every tear from their eyes and they are each able to clearly see their name, which has been formed from the depths of his mercy, lifting each life from the dust. That is our future, brought out from the sorrows of long-established suffering in the world.

"The Rock! His work is perfect, for all His ways are just" (Deut 32:4).

Bibliography

Allen, Ginger. "From Dust to Dust." *Answers in Genesis*, February 15, 2012. https://answersingenesis.org/human-body/from-dust-to-dust/.

Berry, Galia. "The Last Jew of Peki'in." *Aish.com*, June 30, 2018. http://www.aish.com/jw/id/The-Last-Jew-of-Pekiin.html.

Bone, David. "How Flint Is Formed." South Downs National Park Authority State of the National Park 2012. http://snpr.southdowns.gov.uk/files/additions/For%20how%20flint%20is%20formed.htm.

Hazen, Robert. "Life's Rocky Start." PBS, January 13, 2016. http://www.pbs.org/wgbh/nova/earth/life-rocky-start.html.

"How Did Minerals Form in Our Earth?" *UCSB ScienceLine*, April 8, 2013. http://scienceline.ucsb.edu/getkey.php?key=3913.

Jenkins, Aric. "Americans Lonely." *Fortune*, May 1, 2018. http://fortune.com/2018/05/01/americans-lonely-cigna-study/.

Kierkegaard, Soren. *Works of Love*. 1847. Translated by Howard V. Hong. 2nd ed. Princeton, NJ: Princeton University Press, 1995.

King, Hobart M. "Corundum." *Geology.com*. https://geology.com/minerals/corundum.shtml.

Posner, Menachem. "What Does Manna Mean?" *Chabad.org*. https://www.chabad.org/parshah/article_cdo/aid/1410463/jewish/What-Does-Manna-Mean.htm.

Rosenfeld, Dovid. "Covenant of Salt." *Aish.com*, Ask the Rabbi. http://www.aish.com/atr/Covenant-of-Salt.html.

Smith, Colin. "When God Hides You." *Unlocking the Bible*, April 29, 2012. https://unlockingthebible.org/sermon/when-god-hides-you/.

Villanueva, John Carl. "How Are Rocks Formed?" *Universe Today*, December 3, 2009. https://www.universetoday.com/46594/how-are rocks formed/.

www.ingramcontent.com/pod-product-compliance
Lightning Source LLC
Chambersburg PA
CBHW070926160426
43193CB00011B/1589